What an inspiring story of God's love and our hope in Him! God will use this book to encourage many toward a closer walk with their Lord, lead lost people to salvation, and help all who read it be better equipped to remember that even life's harshest tragedy falls under God's sovereign authority, is intertwined with His grace and mercy, and comes wrapped in His love. Mark Canfora's story will help every reader live with an eternal perspective, which is such a message of hope for us all.

> — DEBBIE IN FLORIDA

In this book, you can sense the tender and loving care of two fathers— Mark Canfora and our heavenly Father. The author captured my heart with his heart for God. Clearly, he is a man of God who has been broken by God, and the resulting fruit will bless the lives of many.

> — PAUL IN GEORGIA

This is a powerful book, and I pray that God uses it in miraculous ways.

> — JAMES IN INDIANA

I applaud Mr. Canfora's bold outreach. Parents can be very quiet about this type of pain, even though when we connect, the power of many is a source of great comfort. This work and this message are very much needed.

> — KELLY IN MARYLAND

This is a gripping story—and I love it when God uses tragedy to draw people closer to Him. I'm sad about the tragedy that struck the Canfora family, but what a blessing this book will be!

> — RODNEY IN TENNESSEE

Mark Canfora was anointed to write this book! I know his message will bless and help many, many, many parents who've gone through the same thing. I pray for God's blessings and favor on this book and those who read it.

— MAGDA IN OHIO

I lost my son Trevor on Easter Sunday of 2009 in Panama City, Florida, and Mark Canfora's book touched my heart. I can relate so much to his description of his pain. Trevor was our blue-eyed angel... and he had Down syndrome. The heart and soul of our family, Trevor was all about love, unconditional love. Even in his death, Trevor changed my life. All I could think to do was cry out to Jesus and beg Him to be with me. For the first time ever, I began reading the Bible; I yearned to know God, and I cried with Him, prayed to Him, yelled to Him....and it is only by His grace that I am here today. I just can't thank Mr. Canfora enough for this book... for sharing his story... and for caring about others who are hurting....Thank you! Thank you! Thank you!

– ANGIE IN FLORIDA

Thank you so much for bringing Mark Jr. into all of our lives. You should be proud of him! I will greatly miss him until we meet again. And, Mr. Canfora, thank you for bringing God back into my life!

– MANDY, A HIGH-SCHOOLER IN OHIO

Mark Canfora has found the loving power of God in the deepest valley of his life! A true story of how much God loves us!

– LARRY WAYNE, EVENING HOST, K-LOVE RADIO NETWORK (WWW.KLOVE.COM)

A Child Died, a Father Cried...
and God Answered

A Child Died, a Father Cried...
and God Answered

MARK CANFORA

Read and Believe!
Panama City Beach, Florida

DEDICATION

I dedicate this book especially to God and every other father who has painfully experienced the death of his precious child. This book is also dedicated to all parents, grandparents, siblings, family, and friends who know—or one day will know—the heartache and pain experienced at the death of a child or the passing of a dear loved one.

To my Lord and Savior Jesus Christ, first and foremost, my thanks for giving Your life and shedding Your blood for the forgiveness of our sins. Thank You, Lord, for revealing Yourself to me and being my strength during difficult times.

To my wife, Dena, who is by far the strongest, wisest, most beautiful, and most courageous woman I have been blessed to know. I thank God you came into my life. I am proud to call you my wife and the mother of our beautiful children. And thank you to my mother-in-law, Grandma Linda. You showed me Jesus through your life as well as the amazing daughter you raised.

My daughter, Carly, your strength, beauty, and life are a testimony in itself to the greatness of God. You have inspired me to be a better father and a better man of God. I love you with all my heart. Your love, strength, and encouraging words have helped see me through, and I vow to finish the race. I love you, CC!

To my children, Juliana, Brooke, and Dominic, I have come to realize these past few years what treasures on earth really are: smiles, hugs, kisses, and precious moments between children and their parents. These daily treasures are the simple moments in time at a ballgame, a cheerleading competition, or a gentle kiss goodnight. You all three are gifts from God, and I love you with all my heart.

To my parents, words cannot convey the sacrifice and wisdom you have given our family. I thank God for your sixty-plus years of marriage and for teaching me love beyond measure. God blessed me the day He gave me you as Mom and Dad. I am forever grateful, and I love you both with all my heart.

To my pastor, Mike Guarnieri—a true man of God. Thank you for walking the walk, not just talking the talk. You have earned the honor and privilege to be called "Pastor."

To my closest friends, brothers and sisters in the Lord—Matthew Fetter, Bryan Yurick, Julius Toth, Gina Moon, Nathan Glick, Word of Life Ministries, The Father's House, and Cornerstone Family Fellowship/ PC, Florida. Thank you for showing me love beyond measure.

To Mark Jr.'s and my entire family, brothers Alan and Sonny, sister Chic, aunts, uncles, cousins, and friends—thank you for your love, kindness, and encouragement through the years.

To Mark Jr., my precious son…
    As each day passes here on earth,
    I know that I am one step closer to being together with you
    as we are reunited in heaven.
    Oh, what a glorious day that will be
    when I truly experience what God means by
    storing up treasures in heaven.
    I love you son, with all my heart.
    We will be together again, one fine day.
    .

ACKNOWLEDGMENTS

Thank you to the following people, contributors, and organizations: you helped make this book complete:

Ann and Albert Canfora: my mom and dad. I love you!

Pastor Greg Aldridge and Cornerstone Family Fellowship Church

The Carrs: Jimmy, Susan, Steven, Daniel, and Cristine

The Perrys: Larry, Pam, and Cassie

John and Genell Homner

The Word of Life Street Ministry, Barberton, Ohio

James Watkins and Lisa Guest for their editing skills

Larry Wayne of Larry Wayne Studios for his audio recordings

Eric Walljasper of Eric Walljasper Graphic Design

ACW Press for its help with making this book a reality!

CONTENTS

A WORD FROM THE AUTHOR

Key to any journey in life is to not go it alone. The wisdom of the ages reflects the importance of friends on the rough road each of us walks in this world.

Two are better than one…

If one falls down,

his friend can help him up….

Also, if two lie down together, they will keep warm.

> *But how can one keep warm alone.*

Though one may be overpowered,

two can defend themselves.
ECCLESIASTES 4:9-12 NIV

There is nothing like being overpowered by the loss of a loved one, especially the loss of a child. If you're hurting because of the loss of someone you love, I'm glad you picked up this book. You are not alone. You will find in these pages assurance that others have felt pain like you're feeling and that others have found hope despite its often suffocating stranglehold.

In the appendices at the end of the book, you will find more company—more words of hope as well as tested truths that have helped people walk the difficult path we find ourselves treading when a loved one passes on.

Our Web site is another source of company for your painful journey. You'll find many resources and the ability to connect with people who know something of your pain because they have walked a similar path.

Finally, you may have found company in the Lord Jesus Christ. He has definitely been key to my journey. Even if you haven't introduced yourself to Him yet, keep reading anyway. What you find in these pages will only help you keep putting one foot in front of the other.

Don't travel this road alone! And please contact me if I can come alongside you in any way.

MARK CANFORA
JANUARY 2010

1

At the Park

"Daddy, Marky's dead."

The impact of these words from Carly, my sixteen-year-old daughter, nearly stopped my heart. As life seemed to drain from my body, I gasped for a breath. All I could say was a whispered, "No, no…. Oh, God, no…."

As I sat motionless on the edge of the bed, the phone still pressed to my ear, my mind reeled, and I struggled to breathe. It was as if I had awakened from a horrible, terrible dream. But this was no dream—it was the nightmare that was now my life.

This call is real. I'm not imagining it, I thought, as the chilling words echoed in my ears…. "Daddy, Marky's dead."

"How?" I managed to ask.

Having received a phone call from one of Marky's friends, Carly explained between her sobs. "He hanged himself, Daddy . . . in the pavilion at Edgewood Park. The police and ambulance are here now . . . but they are taking him away."

Dena—my wife, Marky and Carly's stepmother—had awakened. Panicked by the middle-of-the-night phone call and the pain she immediately sensed in me, she cried out, "What happened?" Having helped me raise Mark Jr. since he was five years old, she truly had been like a mother to him.

"Marky's dead," I replied. She sat straight up in bed, and I heard her talking, trying desperately to grasp what I had said. But her words faded as my head spun and I continued to gasp for breath.

WHY?

Picturesque and serene, Edgewood Park is a beautiful twenty-acre park located in Barberton, Ohio. Eighty- to one-hundred-year-old trees line the park, which is spotted with baseball fields, basketball courts, and children's play areas. This lovely place had been the scene of special times and cherished memories. We had shared countless good times of fun and laughter as the children were growing up. We had also enjoyed the peace and tranquility that Edgewood offered.

But now, as I began to live this nightmare, I knew that I would always think of the park—Mark and his friends had called it "The Wood"—as my son's final resting place before he went home to heaven.

I rose to my feet to get dressed and make my way to the park to see my son—or so I thought. In shock, I stumbled out of our bedroom to go be with my son and to comfort my daughter. *What pain she must be in*, I thought. No sixteen-year-old should ever have to make that kind of phone call to her father.

Making my way to the car, I began what I thought would be a twenty-minute drive to the park. But the only thing I remember about that drive was my asking God, "Why? Why, God? Why? I've done the things You've asked me to do. I've obeyed You, Lord! I've been obedient to the best of my limited ability, and I've listened to You. Why, Lord? Why?"

What did I do wrong? What did I do to deserve this? Was Marky's suicide somehow my fault? I don't understand.

As I made my way to the highway, I suddenly realized that I was driving at a dangerous speed and was pretty much out of control. Slowing down a bit, I thought, *What if I go to the park and they're gone? Where would they take Marky?*

I slammed on the brakes and came to a screeching halt. I had stopped in the middle of the highway. It was about three o'clock in the morning, and I felt as if the whole world had stopped and I was the only one out there. Sitting in my car at the intersection of the I-77 Akron South and I-21 Barberton South split and sobbing uncontrollably, I called the Barberton Police Department.

"My son, Mark Jr., just died in the Edgewood Park pavilion. Can you tell me if he is still there?" I murmured.

There was a brief pause on the line. "No, sir, he isn't. They are transporting him to the Summit County coroner's facility." The morgue.

ALL THINGS?

I turned the car toward downtown Akron to go be with my son. During that ten-minute drive, I received the first of God's many responses to my desperate cries for an answer, cries that began early that morning and continued in the months that followed. As various thoughts raced through my mind, I cried out loud to God: "Why? I need to know why! I've given my life to You. I've obeyed Your call on my life. I've done the best I can. How is this ever going be a good thing, God? How?"

I continued my frantic conversation with God. "You said *all things* work together for good for those that believe. I don't see it . . . . How can I live with this pain? . . . I want to die too.... God, help me! Help me, please. . . ."

My eyes filled with tears, and I could not see the road. As the flood of tears rolled down my cheeks, everything was blurred—every physical object before me and every thought and emotion that raced through my mind and heart. "I can't do this. I can't."

I heard the Lord say, "I am with you. I am your strength."

"I'M NOT ALONE"

Then I thought of my elderly parents. *This is going to devastate them. Oh no! What if they hear this on their police scanner? They always have it on. I don't want them to hear about Marky on the scanner, and I don't want anyone else to tell them. The shock could kill them.*

I reached for my cell phone, found my sister Chic's number, and dialed. "Chicky," I cried, waking her from her sleep.

"What? What is it?"

"Marky is dead."

She screamed, "Oh no, Mark! Oh no! What happened?"

"They said he hanged himself at Edgewood Park. He's on his way to the coroner's right now." I asked her to call Alan, our oldest brother. I wanted the two of them to go to Mom and Dad and let them know.

"Where are you?" she shouted.

"I'm on my way to the coroner's to be with Marky."

"No, Marky! Don't go." Even though I was forty-seven years old, I was still Marky to my older sister. "You can't do this alone. Wait for me."

"I'm not alone, Chicky," I struggled to say between sobs. "Jesus is with me."

Even in the suffocating pain, I knew God's voice when He spoke, "I am your strength." And even in the darkness of unimaginable grief, I knew God's Son, Jesus Christ. I felt His strength at that moment.

"Please, just go to Mom and Dad's, and I'll be there later," I told my sister.

2

At the Coroner's Office

As I drove down the street to the coroner's office, I could see an ambulance in the parking lot. I parked my car on the street and ran toward the vehicle. The paramedics, lowering the gurney from the back, were startled when I cried out, "I think that's my son—Mark Canfora."

They looked at me with heartfelt compassion in their eyes and said, "Yes. Yes, this is your son. But, sir, are you sure you want to do this?"

"Yes," I said softly as I looked at the outline of my son's body inside the body bag. "I have to be with my son."

The medical examiner came from the building and asked the same question: "Sir, are you sure you want to do this?"

"Yes," I said adamantly. "I have to be with my child."

I walked beside them as they wheeled my son into the building. Once inside, I stood there silently, motionless, staring at this black body bag where my child, my little boy, my Marky now lay.

ALONE WITH MY SON

"I'll get you a chair," I heard someone say.

Then, alone with my son, I quickly unzipped the body bag. There, lying before me, was my son… in basketball shorts and socks. No shirt. But resting gently on his chest were Mom and Dad's WWII dog tags that he'd always worn around his neck.

Then I saw the rope burn, scarred onto his neck, and he looked as if he were sleeping. With my finger, I traced the outside of the burn on his neck, the exact place where the rope had squeezed the life out of him. Marky's eyes were half open, just as I had seen them many other times when he slept. *This can't be real*, I thought. *This is my baby, my son.* He had been so full of life one moment... and utterly lifeless the next.

Almost automatically, I placed my hands on his chest. "Jesus, I want my son back. Please breathe life back into him."

"He's not here." I heard a voice I had never heard before. It was not audible to the world. Only in my Spirit and in my mind.

With tears, I quickly responded, "I know he's not here, but I want him back, Jesus!"

I know this body is his earthly tent, I thought. I again laid my hands firmly on Marky's chest and prayed, "Lord, breathe life into my son. Please let him live."

Truly believing that Jesus was going to raise my child, I watched for breath to re-enter his body. With great anticipation, I watched for Marky to breathe again. I stood there—motionless, believing, watching. After all, the Bible says that if we have the faith of a mustard seed, we can move mountains—and this was the greatest mountain of my life. So I asked God once again to raise him.

I searched for Scripture verses to pray. "You raised Lazarus, You raised the centurion's servant, You raised Jairus's little girl from the dead. Marky is surely as worthy as the centurion's servant, Lord. Please raise him, God. Please."

And then God answered. "You asked for his life, and I gave it to you. Now he is with me."

BY GOD'S GRACE

What happened at that moment was like nothing I had ever before experienced... I was taken back eighteen-and-a-half years to 1986 and the day Marky was born. Akron General Hospital was only blocks from where I presently stood, and I clearly saw myself kneeling on a hallway floor there, begging God and praying with everything in me to let my baby son live.

Marky had almost died in the hospital the day he was born. It was just after 4:30 a.m., and Marky was coming too fast. The charts, fetal monitor, and other machines screamed, "Trauma!" The umbilical cord was wrapped around his neck. The neonatal nurse had run into our birthing room and begun trying to prevent his birth by placing her hand on top of his crowning head. When the doctors arrived, they put Marky's mom to sleep to keep her from pushing. My wife was in trouble, and my baby was choking and unable to breathe.

The doctors and nurse ordered me to stay put as they wheeled my now unconscious wife and unborn child to a different room, but I didn't stay put. Our baby was lodged in the birth canal, and nothing—no one—could keep me from following my wife and my baby!

I watched the doctors bolt through two large double doors that swung back and forth vigorously after they passed. I wedged my foot between the doors so I could hear what was being said, and I looked through the small panes of glass as they desperately tried to save our child's life. After a few seconds passed, I eased into the room. Standing some thirty feet away from the unfolding drama, I watched, prayed, and begged God to let my baby live.

Marky was delivered several minutes later at 4:56 a.m. He was somewhat motionless after the umbilical cord was removed from around his neck, and he didn't cry immediately as newborns usually do. Marky had been delivered with forceps, and they had given him oxygen right away. Then the nurse screamed, "He's not moving!" They suctioned his mouth and nose and gave him oxygen. Then, within moments after the oxygen mask was removed from his little face, Marky began to cry. By God's grace, I had my son.

I HAD A SON!

"It's a boy," the nurse said quietly.

But the drama wasn't over. Another nurse frantically shouted, "His left side isn't moving, Doctor. His left side!"

The doctor shouted an order, and the nurse rubbed his body vigorously. Marky let out another cry, and this one rocked the entire hospital. Still, my desperate prayers continued: this father begged his heavenly Father to allow his son to live.

The nurse looked my way and gently asked, "Doctor, do you think it's all right if the father comes over to see his son now?"

I know none of them had seen me standing there until the emergency procedure was over. And, gracious, kind, and relieved that our baby lived, they said nothing about the fact that I had disobeyed their order to stay put.

I was in awe, overwhelmed with thanks and appreciation. I had a son. I thanked God, the doctors, and the nurses. I cried as I held my Marky.

BEFORE AND AFTER

Before September 8, 1986, I was self-centered and immature. I had felt no need for God in most areas of my life. Only occasionally, when I wanted something or when I was in trouble, would I turn to Him. I was like most people who don't have a relationship with God. I talked to Him when I wanted something from Him.

I was so undeserving of a loving God, but He answered my prayers when I cried out to Him in those early-morning hours. This twenty-eight-year-old husband and, now, new father didn't know God, but He knew me. And He answered my desperate cry and let Marky live. God blessed me with what turned out to be 6,870 precious days with my child, my son.

As Marky's birth day unfolded, his mother Gina soon awoke from the anesthetics to discover we had a son. In fact, she was the last member of the family to find out that good news. Her parents, my parents, aunts, uncles, and the rest of the family all heard my exuberant shouts of "It's a boy, it's a boy! I have my Marky! It's a boy!"

IN A NEW PLACE

On the evening of September 8, as I drove home to our apartment... located right across the street from Edgewood Park... I was thanking God and crying with joy. The closer I got to the apartment, the more I cried. I felt drained and completely alone. I wanted my wife... I wanted my son....

As God would have it, I reached out to Him that evening. Oh, I had reached out to Him earlier in the day, and He had revealed Himself to me in a most miraculous way. God had created life in my son: I had witnessed the miracle of Marky's birth and God's powerful answer to my prayers for his life to be spared.

God continued to reveal His love for me while I sat in my car in the lot sandwiched between our apartment—Marky's first home—and the park where he would later take his last breath.

And, oddly, a message on the Christian radio station was playing in the background that night. I usually listened to rock and roll, not anything Christian. I don't recall specifics about the message, but I do remember hearing about the loving sacrifice of Christ and how much God loves us. I cried as I sat behind the wheel of my car. I was in a new place,

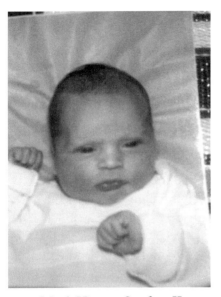

Mark Vincent Canfora II
Born September 8, 1986, 4:56 A.M.

Mark Sr. and Mark Jr. 1987

Mark Canfora Jr., 1986–2005
My son and my treasure in heaven

even though it had lasted for only a moment in time. I finished listening to the message and went to bed.

GOD KNEW*

In His infinite knowledge and wisdom, God knew what was ahead of me. He knew that the next eighteen-and-a-half years would be but a vapor, a mist in God's eternity.

He knows the end from the beginning and the beginning from the end. God truly knows all—past, present, and future.[1]

And when I asked this all-knowing God for my baby son's life, He gave it to me. But now Marky was with the Lord in heaven. I knew at that moment Marky was not coming back, and a peace that passes all human understanding filled me that early morning as I experienced a profound gratitude that God had already answered my prayer to let Marky live. Marky now lived with God Himself in heaven, and he would be there for eternity.[2]

Now, in the coroner's office, I had some precious minutes to say good-bye to Marky. Good-bye for now, but not forever.

TOTAL RELIANCE ON GOD

My life would be different from this point on. Why? Because I was—at last—in the place where God wants us to all to live: in total reliance on Him.

I now knew that I needed God more than I needed anything or anyone else in the world. I knew I could not live or survive this onslaught of hopelessness, fear, bitterness, and pain without God. These indescribable and excruciating emotions were not of God. Tragedy had brought me to this crossroads, and I was choosing—and I would continue to choose— to live and abide in Christ, to walk out my life spiritually. The alternative

---

* Superscripted numbers begin appearing in this section. They point you to endnotes and Scripture verses in Appendix A, "Truth for My Journey—and Yours." Appendices D, "God's Promises About Our Children and Loved Ones in Heaven," and E, "More Words of Life," also contain important passages from God's Word. Also listed in Appendix D—and available to listen to on our Web site—are songs that have been a source of truth, comfort, and hope for me. I encourage you to read through the final pages of this book and to listen to the songs I've listed for you.

was to suffer through the rest of my days on this earth in the worst pain and agony imaginable.

To be honest, over the next several days, I journeyed back and forth between these two realities—God's peace and suffocating pain—and I did so from moment to moment, from hour to hour.

The battle was on, though, and many lives were at stake—spiritually as well as literally.

God answered the cry of a twenty-eight-year-old father that September morning in 1986 at Akron General Hospital and his son would live.

> God knew the day Marky was born, and, at the same time, God knew the day Marky would be taken home to heaven. What I didn't know then, but now know to be true, is this: God loves us unconditionally. He knows the hairs numbered on our heads. He knows us all by name. He knows the day we are born and the day we will die.[3]

Standing there in the coroner's building, I knew my son was not coming back to life on this earth. I knew, though, that he was very much alive in heaven with his Lord.

Reaching deep into my memory, I thought back to October 7, 2000, the day fourteen-year-old Marky came to me and said, "Daddy, I'm ready to accept Jesus as my Savior." And we prayed. I was at peace and very glad as I praised and thanked God. Marky was saved. My family was saved.

Now, as I stood there in the coroner's office, I clung to the hope and promise from God that Marky was in heaven.

3

At the Park with Carly

I called Carly after I left the coroner's office and told her I was on my way to Edgewood. In tears, she said, "Daddy, about twenty of our friends are here, and they're all upset and crying." She continued, "And, Daddy, I'm worried about Mom. And somebody said God must hate us."

"Oh no, Carly," I replied. "I'll tell you when I get there—and I'll tell your mom and the others, too—that we are truly loved by God. And we were blessed to have Marky for the time God gave us."

As I drove to the park, I was praising and thanking God for the precious gift of my children. I continued that line of thought with Carly: "We are going to celebrate Marky's life. We will celebrate how much God loved us and how He showed that love by letting us have Marky for the time we had with him here on earth. And God will show us His love by letting us have time with Marky in heaven for eternity."

I was excited about sharing this new revelation about how much God really does love us. He *is* a loving God. When tragic events happen and when we find ourselves walking in the valley, God doesn't hate us, and neither are we cursed by Him. God gives us the precious gift of life. God is the ultimate Gift-Giver. He gives for a season, and sometimes, for unknown reasons, He takes away.

NO ONE'S FAULT

As I arrived at Edgewood Park around 5:00 a.m., I found a large gathering of young people, but at that moment the only person I wanted to see was Carly. I hugged her, and she hugged me harder than I had ever been hugged before. She was scared, hurting, confused, and crying—as were all of Carly and Marky's friends.

We stood under the streetlights in the park where all of us had experienced so much joy and fun; it was the site of such good times and great memories. I gathered the kids around and inwardly asked God for the right words to say to them. Marky's girlfriend, Kristina, and his best friend, Jason, were there, along with many more friends.

I asked everyone to join hands and, before I prayed, I spoke gently: "There will be no finger-pointing. This is nobody's fault. God knew the day Marky would be born—and the day Marky would go home to heaven. Again, this is no one's fault."

Then I prayed and thanked God for the gift of life in Mark, Jr., and how God had saved his life at birth. I thanked Him for Marky's new life in Christ when, at age fourteen, he named Jesus as his Savior and Lord. And I acknowledged that the timing of Marky's death truly was God's will: He planned the day when Marky would be born, and He planned the day when Marky would be at peace in heaven. Marky's death was not the result of a fight with his girlfriend or a misunderstanding with a friend: nobody caused this. I wanted everyone there to know freedom from guilt as well as freedom from Satan's lies and accusations.

I then spent time with Marky's mom and pointed out the love that God had shown us when He blessed us with Marky's life that day in Akron General Hospital. I reminded her that Marky was a precious gift from a loving God, and she agreed. She knew that Marky had loved her with all his heart. Her son always greeted her with a kiss and an "I love you."

A MEASURE OF GOD'S LOVE

But how do we measure God's love when we don't understand why He has allowed something difficult—a tragedy or pain beyond description—to happen to us? I found it helpful to look at the precious gift of life, of love, that God has given each of us in our children. The miracle of birth is a gift of love.

Still, what would any parents give to have just one more day with a child who has passed away before they did! What would they give? Ask any one of them; ask me; ask yourself. What would we give? Anything! And everything! We would give everything we own, all that we have, and anything we ever would own for just one more day, one more hour, or even one more minute to hold our child once again! Anything and everything in order to hug and kiss, to hear the words "I love you, Daddy" or "I love you, Mommy," or to say, "I love you, son."

I saw real evidence of God's love for me in the 6,870 days God let Marky live after I cried out to Him for Marky's life that early September morning in 1986. He could have died on that birthing table, but God let him live those precious days we were blessed with. Marky's life was indeed a measure of God's love for me.

After all, for those of us who believe that Jesus is God's Son and who have accepted Him as our Lord and Savior, God promises everlasting life in heaven with our children who pass on before us.[4]

ALL CHILDREN GO TO HEAVEN

Our children in heaven are part of our future, not our past.

And you can be confident of that. After all, God is a God of justice, love, and mercy. Knowing Him, I believe that when children die before reaching an age of accountability—an age when they are mentally and psychologically able to choose to name Jesus as their Savior—then God will, out of His abundant grace and mercy, welcome those children into heaven for eternity (see 2 Samuel 12:23; Matthew 18:3-6, 19:14). It doesn't matter if the child was raised as a Muslim, Hindu, Buddhist, or atheist. Angels take all children who die too soon into Jesus' arms upon their death.[5]

In Marky's case, he went home to the Lord at eighteen-and-a-half years of age. I was confident that he was with Jesus because Marky had freely and willingly given his life to the Lord when he was fourteen; it had been his choice, his own decision. He is saved, so he is in my eternal future. The Bible says it, and that is the final word for me and for those who know God and know He never lies. God is faithful and His promises are true.

But there's more. Our children already in heaven want one thing—and one thing only: for their parents, siblings, family members, and friends to join them there. That's it. Their desire is that everyone they know and love comes to know Jesus Christ as their Lord and Savior and, in God's time, to have their family and friends join them in heaven.

This is my message to parents who survive the death of a child. I reaffirm for these hurting moms and dads what we believers know to be true: our children await us in heaven.

And what a hope-filled message for unbelievers as well as believers! For unbelievers to hear that their child is alive in heaven and can be a part of their future should they choose to accept Jesus Christ as their Lord and Savior—these words of healing and hope seem too good to be true to grieving parents. But that *is* the truth: God has prepared a place for our children and for us. If our children pass before we do, they want nothing else but for us to join them in heaven... by God's grace and in His appointed time.[6]

4

Eighteen-and-a-Half Years Earlier

As I stood over my child's body there in the morgue, how did I have enough faith in God to lay hands over Mark's unbeating heart and ask Jesus Christ to let him live?

Was this just another I-need-God moment? Was this merely the next I'm-in-trouble-and-I-can't-fix-it-myself situation?

Or had I, by God's grace, developed a deeper relationship with Him? And if so, what path had I taken since that day eighteen-and-a-half years earlier when I was on my knees begging a God I didn't even know to let my baby live?

RUNNING AND FEARING

When Marky passed, I was forty-seven years old, and I had given my life fully to the Lord some eight years earlier. At that remarkable moment, I truly experienced what Christians describe as "being born again." (Other ways to describe salvation are *conversion* and *new birth*.) By the grace of God, I had survived a thirty-nine-year journey of a pretentious and confused, on-again off-again relationship with God. I typically turned to Him in times of trouble, need, or want, but I never really knew Him or even tried to develop the kind of personal relationship with Him that He created us to enjoy—and that He so much desires to share with each of us.

Oh, I always felt that God had a plan for my life, but I just didn't fully understand all that this truth means. I was first introduced to God and

Jesus through a local church and then again later by several overzealous, religious people asking me, "Do you have a personal relationship with Jesus? Without Jesus as your Savior, you will burn in hell!" I definitely didn't experience any sense of love from those people, so with my background and then this negative experience with "religion," I wanted no part of their Christianity. In fact, most of the religion I had been exposed to would make anyone run as far away as possible from God and Jesus. And that is exactly what I did from age twelve to age thirty-six.

I had begrudgingly attended a local church until I was twelve years old, and most of the time I would have rather been at home with my dad or playing football with my buddies. Most of the time I was at church, I was totally confused—and really afraid of God. That church had so many rules and regulations. The Ten Commandments were tough enough to follow, but the church's rules—which I later learned were not anywhere in the Bible but were instead man-made—were even tougher to obey. For instance, simply touching the wafer—the host—at communion with my hands was a mortal sin that would keep me out of heaven if I didn't confess it to the priest before I died... The only way to heaven also required me to get in the confessional booth each week and confess my mortal sins, venial sins, and any and every other type of sin to the priest sitting behind the wire screen.... I never heard much about reading the Bible or talking to God or Jesus.... Coming before God by way of the priest was the only hope for a sinner.... So I went to church out of fear, not reverence and definitely not love.

I hope I haven't lost any readers, because I do believe that many churches like the one I attended have since changed several of these man-made rules, that members of the congregation do reverence God, they do read their Bibles, and they do have a personal relationship with Him through Jesus Christ. But I'm getting ahead of myself....

"YOUR ORDER, PLEASE"

I was twelve years old on May 4, 1970, the day my oldest brother was shot and wounded at Kent State University during an anti-war demonstration. This tragedy consumed much of our family's lives over the next several years. The priest from our church stopped by our home a few days after the shootings. One afternoon, after a heated disagreement about the tragedy, my mother asked the priest to leave our home, and we never attended church again.

That's when I began the stage of my life's journey outside of and away from the church. I believed in God, but my god was a fast-food, short-order-chef type. If I wanted something, I'd ask God. If I needed something, I'd ask God. If I were in trouble or scared, I'd ask God.

No relationship.

No real gratitude.

No nothing.

When things are good, who needs God?

That was my pattern in life… from age twelve through age thirty-six. I knew God was out there somewhere, but I was quite content doing whatever pleased me; the lusts of the flesh were my gods.[7]

ENCOUNTERS WITH DEATH

The fear of death, however, confronted me on occasions: uncles, aunts, and even a thirty-two-year-old cousin suddenly died. And these funerals were hard: We all had to face the reality of our own death and the haunting fact that one day each one of us will die and begin spending eternity—forever and ever and ever—somewhere….

The question of whether I would spend eternity in hell or heaven bothered me, but that issue—thanks to the enemy—seemed hopelessly confusing. I didn't realize I was just one simple prayer away from determining my eternal future and choosing heaven as my destination.

God's grace, God's forgiveness, the place He reserves for His children in heaven—all these and much more are free gifts from Him through His Son Jesus Christ. There was nothing I had to do—nothing I could do—to earn God's love and favor. But only later would I learn the truth that all my works and efforts to make it into heaven were fruitless. Only later would I discover that we are saved by God's grace; that I simply had to receive what He offered.[8]

But in the meantime, like most people, I tried not to think about death and what happens afterward. I was young and naïve. And I definitely had no room for God in my life. I somehow knew—or thought I knew—that His presence would cramp my sinful lifestyle. Life as I was living it was all about me, and the purpose of my days on this earth was, as far as I was concerned, to get all I could for me. It was a philosophy of selfish living at its finest. For me, it was a life guided and fueled by pride. And I have come to realize that pride is a killer because it interferes with what God has created all of us for: relationship with Him.

What I later learned—the hard way, of course—was that money, sex, possessions, accomplishments, and relationships could never, ever satisfy me completely. Total peace and joy would always be elusive on the path I was walking. Oh, I knew temporary happiness and random moments of fun, but those feelings and experiences soon faded away.

Like most people living for themselves, I always thought, *There's got to be more to life than this.* And there was, but I could only realize that if I were willing to die to myself and to my sinful, selfish nature. And slowly, unwillingly, and with much pain and heartache, I did exactly that.

HITTING ROCK BOTTOM

After Mom asked the priest to leave our home, we left the church, and I had a great life growing up in Barberton, a town that loved its sports teams as much as its industry.

Baseball was my first love, and I played with passion through high school and then at the University of Akron. I even received an invitation to try out for the big leagues with the Cleveland Indians in the old Municipal Stadium on Lake Erie.

I met Marky and Carly's mother during my college days, and we were married in the early eighties. After college, I got into sales and marketing, which meant traveling the country and a salesman's life on the road.

The fourteen years of traveling, entertaining customers, and drinking led to several personal problems, one of which was alcoholism. A looming divorce from Marky and Carly's mother in the early nineties, some bad business decisions, and an unscrupulous partner who stole lots of money from me led to further drinking binges.

I hit rock bottom… and I was only thirty-three.

But God didn't let me stay there. He had a different plan for my life, so at this point He simply removed all the things in my life that had been my gods: money, my career, and all the worldly stuff I had accumulated.

The bright spot in this dark season? I had always been a great dad, and I had always shown my children heartfelt unconditional love. I loved life and was great to be around—as long as things were going my way. The loving dad part of me never changed, but all the rest did….

I was now divorced, and my drinking problem worsened. My life was miserable, and I was angry at the world.

At age thirty-three, I truly thought my life was pretty much over, and

I was really feeling sorry for myself. I considered ending it all. I had set up the life insurance policy and convinced myself that my children would be better off without me.

That's when God sent my wife Dena—and her warm and contagiously Christian mom—into my life.

BAD TO WORSE

After about a year, Dena and I moved in together, and she became pregnant with my third child, Juliana. We were unmarried at the time.

I continued to drink, and my alcohol problem grew progressively worse....

During the first couple of years Dena and I lived together, though, I often asked her mother about her faith in God and her relationship with Jesus. She always had a good answer, and she always backed it up with the Bible.

Most of her responses made sense to me, but what I really wanted were her confidence and inner peace. Every time I asked about that peace, her answer was always the same: "It comes from Jesus." She was always reading the Bible and going to church. And I noticed that it was a package deal in her life: Jesus, Bible reading, and church. Not just one or two, but all three....

The bottom was dropping out from under me, and I really was miserable. After I had another bad episode of binge drinking with the boys, Dena told me she was leaving, and I willingly moved her back to her mother's house with our one-year-old daughter.

I pridefully thought to myself, *I don't need her. I don't need anybody.* I resumed my weekend binge and then headed back on the road to southern Ohio. I had a job selling steel to the mining industry.

I was well aware that my trip would take me along a mountain road—cliff side. How convenient! I could easily make my death look like an accident, and the $500,000 life insurance policy named my children as beneficiaries. It was all laid out before me. As far as I was concerned, my life was over; I had hit rock bottom. I thought, *I am a failure and a loser. My family is better off with me dead.*

I know now that the devil had me right where he wanted me: about to be gone from this world and forever in hell.

I was about to be forever separated from my Creator God and from my family. Satan's role on this earth is to prevent God's purpose, desire, and will for us from being fulfilled in our lives. Satan wants to kill and destroy.

Satan is also the father of all lies and the "accuser of the brethren" (Revelation 12:10). Satan had been the leader over all of worship in heaven, but he and one-third of the angels rebelled against God and were cast out. Now Satan is busy on Planet Earth. In the words of Peter, "[our] enemy the devil prowls around like a roaring lion looking for someone to devour" (1 Peter 5:8). And he had found me.[9]

TO LIVE OR DIE?

I was lying on my bed in my room at the Red Roof Inn in St. Clairsville, Ohio, that rainy Monday afternoon of May 23, 1994. Unaware that Satan was feeding me these ideas, I had been convinced that my life was over and that my kids would be better off if I were dead.

I wept uncontrollably for hours, still hungover from the weekend binge and totally sick of my life. I believed I was a failure, and my tears were for my three children I was about to leave behind. Marky was seven, Carly was five, and Juliana had just turned one.

Reaching out to God in desperation, I asked Him to forgive me for what I was about to do. Then I considered calling someone for help, but who? For months I had considered making a call to Alcoholics Anonymous, and I decided to look in the phone book for an AA listing. An eighty-year-old Christian man answered the phone, and he talked to me for a long time. He explained to me not only how much my family needed me but also that I could get help if I would just go to the men's AA meeting starting in an hour just a few miles down the road in the basement of a church in Bridgeport, Ohio. I attended that meeting, and for the first time ever I publicly admitted my drinking problem. I knew in my heart that God was the "higher power" they talked about—and that I needed Him to help me.

As I drove westward on I-70 back to my hotel room, it was dusk... about 8:30 or 9:00 p.m., and the sun's light burst through the clouds for the first time on that rainy Monday. I was greatly encouraged, and one reason was the amazing people I had met that night. I prayed to God and thanked Him.

Suddenly I felt His warmth and presence all around me. At that very moment I knew—unshakably in my heart of hearts—that God was real and that I was done with drinking forever. I called Dena and told her the news, and understandably she responded with skepticism. I could hear a faint "Uh huh." Then she hung up the phone saying, "We'll see."

We reconciled later that week, and I stopped traveling immediately. Dena and I started our real estate company, and I began my healing journey. Dena soon became pregnant again with Brooke, our second child (my fourth), and that's when I proposed marriage to her. We were married on October 9, 1994. To this day my wife is the most beautiful woman I know—both inside and out. She is full of joy and has wisdom beyond her years. I will always love her, and I will be forever thankful to the Lord for bringing Dena into my life.

Not long after I married her wonderful daughter, my mother-in-law, Linda, was diagnosed with cancer and, at just forty-four years of age, given six months to live. She moved in with us, and that's when God started to reveal Himself to me through her life—and I would never be the same person after God gave me that time with her in our home.

Many of my wife's family and friends quickly and unquestioningly accepted the bad news that Linda was going to die. In fact, several of them sat in our living room and talked about what would happen after she was gone. Basically, they sat there planning her imminent funeral, and I listened in disbelief at their lack of faith.

Linda, however, with the Holy Spirit as her companion, simply walked out into the backyard and raked leaves as she prayed to Jesus. God was moving...and I was privileged to see Linda live out her solid faith in her God. I quietly observed the Scriptures about healing and faith that she placed all over her bedroom walls. I watched this brave woman battle cancer without ever shedding a tear or showing an ounce of fear to anyone around her.

I desperately wanted what she had: her faith, her strength, her peace, her love for Jesus. I knew she had something real—she had the peace and faith I was missing in my life, peace and faith I had never seen before. And I wanted it.[10]

I HAD GOD, BUT I DIDN'T HAVE JESUS

During the time from May 23, 1994, the date of my sobriety, until May 31, 1997 when I accepted Jesus as my Lord and Savior (more about this later!), I had God, but I didn't have Jesus. During this three-year period, there probably weren't many days that I didn't talk to God or pray. But I didn't know about talking to Jesus or having a relationship with Him...

I had thought that quitting alcohol and believing in God would bring the peace and joy in my life that had been missing: the God-shaped void within me had almost been filled. But only almost. I was close; I wasn't there yet....

I walked across the street to the park and asked God why He would take Linda away from us. She was the only one in this extended family of ours whose life was an example worthy of following—and that was because she was truly walking with the Lord. *God*, I explained to Him in case He'd missed this crucial fact, *we need her among us! We can't lose her!*

As I looked up to the heavens, I asked God why again and again. *Why would You take Gramma Linda? Why so soon?* And He spoke to me in what had become a wonderfully familiar voice: "She doesn't have to die."

TRYING TO GET RIGHT WITH GOD

Now don't get me wrong. It took me awhile to get used to this voice. After all, I had only had a minimal relationship with God. I saw something I wanted in Linda's relationship with Him and in the lives of a few other believers He sent into my life.

I also had had only limited exposure to the Bible. On occasion, when I would drunkenly stumble back into my hotel room after a long night of drinking, I had read chapters in the book of Mark in the Gideon Bible. I was sure that if God had a word for me, it would be in the Gospel of Mark!

And my prayer life had been limited as well. I prayed like this: "Well, God, I quit drinking but I still feel so incomplete. What's that all about? Something is still missing in my life. Help me."

Still trying to figure out my life with God, I had started some serious social work and was using my double-car garage as a warehouse for the poor. Each month I gave clothing, food, bikes, and toys to the kids in a local housing project. I would make lump-sum offers at garage sales in the city's most affluent areas and buy all the remaining children's items. I then had two box-truck vans pick up all my purchases and haul the gifts to the poor.

The Norton Homes Housing Project was the poorest area in our town and my personal mission field. It was located on the same street where I grew up and where most of my childhood friends had lived as well. And I would estimate that 80 percent of those friends of mine who grew up in those housing projects are, to this day, severely addicted to drugs or alcohol, imprisoned, or dead....

I was going to make a difference in that community so other kids had better options and greater opportunities. You see, I mistakenly believed that I could earn a place in heaven by doing good works and being a good person.[11] I was trying hard to get right with God, and this social work really did feel good—for that day and that day only, though. The next day the good feeling was gone. My good deed was like a fix or a drink to calm the nerves, so I would again ask God, "Why do I still feel so empty?"[12] I was still waiting on His answer to that particular question... but I had gotten a clear answer to my question about Linda.

ACTING ON GOD'S ANSWER

Standing alone in the park and looking up toward heaven, I had asked, "What do you mean 'she doesn't have to die'?"

And I heard God clearly respond: "Get another opinion."

I hurriedly walked back across the street, into the house, and in between all the people still freaking out over the news that Linda had six months to live. My wife and Linda were the only ones acting calm. Dena knew the faith her mother had, and as Dena later put it, "My mom wasn't afraid, so neither was I."

I walked into my office in our home and called the Cleveland Clinic to schedule an appointment for another opinion. It was a Sunday afternoon, and I didn't expect to get anyone with decision-making power to be there. But the ultimate Decision Maker—God Himself—had already decided. He was a step ahead of me, and He directed my path that day.

When the phone was answered, I was transferred to the cancer center. I asked if I could bring my mother-in-law in as soon as possible for a second opinion. When I explained about the six-month terminal diagnosis from our local hospital, I know the person on the other end sensed the urgency of my request. She replied, "Can you have her here Tuesday morning at 9:00 a.m.?"

Several weeks later, in an unprecedented radical surgery, doctors removed lymph nodes and half of a lung. They also performed the dangerous procedure of shaving her aorta. By God's grace, Grandma Linda still lives for Christ and is cancer-free fourteen years later. I love her and I am grateful for the ways she is a great witness of faith in God and His power and love. I owe much to her, and I will be forever grateful to the Lord for blessing me with Linda.

ONE MORE THOUGHT

In hospitals, in nursing homes, and at the scene of an accident, even people who don't believe in God will, on their deathbed, utter "Oh, God!" as their final words.

What will you say? What will your last words be? I pray that mine, spoken in all reverence and hope and completely without fear, will be "Oh, God, into Your hands I commit my Spirit." May those be your last words as well. I'm sure they will be Linda's.

5

In the Valley of the Shadow of Death

I had heard the promise before, Jesus' statement that "In My Father's house are many mansions… I go to prepare a place for you" (John 14:2).

I also knew Jesus' proclamation "I am the way, the truth, and the life. No one comes to the Father except through Me" (verse 6).

I had heard the glorious description of heaven: "God will wipe away every tear from their eyes; there shall be no more death, nor sorrow, nor crying. There shall be no more pain, for the former things have passed away" (Revelation 21:4).[13]

And Peter's statement that "with the Lord one day is as a thousand years, and a thousand years as one day" (2 Peter 3:8) was a paradox I'd always marveled at. God's spiritual time doesn't pass at the same pace that a believer's time does. And we simply don't operate on spiritual time.

In the middle of the night on July 12, 2005 and throughout the surreal early-morning hours, all these words took on a far greater significance for me than I ever could have expected….

If you've lost someone you love, maybe those words are especially meaningful to you as well. After all, you and I may live another five, ten, twenty, or thirty years apart from those loved ones who have gone to our Father's house before us, but in God's *eternal time*, that span is like the passage of only a few moments

And if you've lost people you love, isn't it wonderful to know that they are experiencing no more pain and no more tears? All the sorrow, heartache, and hurt they knew here on earth—they remember none of it.

Those truths give us much to celebrate even in the valley of death's shadow. Perhaps that's why "A Celebration of Life and a Message of Hope in Jesus Christ" was birthed that early morning at Edgewood Park. I made a vow to God that I would share this message—that I would encourage people to celebrate not only the life on this earth that He has blessed us with but also His hope-filled promise of eternity in heaven with Him.

I know that I will tearfully share this story of Marky's death through ministry for the rest of my life, but I will also share with tears of joy the hope I have in God: "Those who sow in tears shall reap in joy" (Psalms 126:5). God placed it in my heart that I am to share with the broken-hearted the love of God and this message of hope in Jesus Christ.[14]

A SHEPHERD IN THE VALLEY

Three days after Marky's death, I was to speak at his funeral, and I knew I wanted an altar call to follow a bold message about a Father who purposely chose to let His Son die, who purposely chose to let His Son be beaten, bruised, pierced, and nailed to a cross to suffer and die for us—and to *rise again!* I wanted to communicate that Jesus will always be there for us: He always hears our prayers and answers them; He gives us hope during life's most difficult and senselessly tragic times; and that He has given us a great Counselor—the gift of the Holy Spirit. When we accept Jesus as our Savior and invite Him to be Lord of our life, we receive the indwelling of the Holy Spirit to guide, comfort, and direct us and to strengthen and encourage us in times of trouble, heartache, and persecution.

The Holy Spirit often uses God's Word to guide and encourage, to show us—at least this was my experience—first that we are messed up and lost on our own and then to lead and empower us for His better way. And this truth offered me a solid foundation during those days of pain beyond description, those days when I came to know all too well that the valley of the shadow of death is a very real place. But God walked with me through it, especially during the three days after Marky's passing. I was definitely in that valley—and maybe you are there now—but I was not alone and neither are you. God was with me as my Shepherd, and He is there *for* you and *with* you as well.[15]

LIFE AND DEATH

Jesus was and continues to be my strength, and the Holy Spirit who lives inside me intercedes for me when I can only moan and groan, when

I am barely able to take a breath or move forward a single step. I am a conqueror: and by the grace of God and in His strength, I can make it through anything and everything.

Again, all these truths came more real than ever during those initial days after Marky's death, those days when I thought, *I cannot live another day, another minute. Not with this pain....* I continually searched for truth from Scripture that would numb the pain and offset the attack of Satan and his demons on my mind and body.

You see, I had entered the ultimate battle for my spiritual—and my physical—life. I now realize it was also a battle for the lives of thousands of people who would come to accept Christ through the message of hope and healing God gave me to share after Marky died. As I came to recognize the battle more clearly, I prayed that millions would be encouraged by this message of hope: I knew Marky was in heaven. I also knew this was spiritual warfare—the passing of my child and the never-ending, relentless attack on my family—and the real battle was being waged in the spiritual realm. And I knew the ending of the story: I knew we are victorious in Christ. And I knew that the only weapon of warfare I could use was, according to Scripture, our sword: the Word of God. I needed to cling to the truth I knew from God's Word—and to cling to the Author of that truth, God Himself—if I were to make it through this valley.

You see, when we are in one of life's horrifying and painful valleys, you and I have a choice to make. I chose that early morning—and countless times through the next three days—to make God my refuge even though much of the time I could hardly breathe, speak, or function. Satan not only had a hand in the death of my child, but he wanted me dead too! So I chose God to be my fortress, my strength, and my hope.

I was about to enter the most difficult and dangerous battle of my life, one that was unlike any other battle I had ever faced. I had fought as an athlete on ball fields, I had battled the insidious enemy of alcohol, I had struggled with the pain of divorce, and I had warred against curses and habitual sins handed down in my family from generation to generation. But the confrontation that occurred in the valley of the shadow of death was a life-and-death battle. Yet as I chose to trust and obey what I had learned from God's Word, I experienced His presence and faithfulness as never before....[16]

THE PAVILION IN THE PARK

After I spent about an hour with Carly, Marky's friends, and Marky and Carly's mother, I walked the five hundred yards toward the pavilion to get more answers from God. *Where did it happen? How did it happen? Why did it happen?* I wanted to know Marky's frame of mind. I needed answers to all my questions about this sudden and tragic turn of events.

With tears streaming down my face, I walked toward the pavilion. The sun had risen above the horizon and given the park a surreal feel. At that point, I recalled the medical examiner's words after I had said good-bye to Marky....

As we both stood over Marky's body lying on the gurney, he said, "You know, I believe half the kids I see come in here like this—death by apparent suicide with a rope or belt—don't intentionally mean to be here at all."

I looked at him with eyes that begged to understand more.

"In a few short seconds—just two or three—they pass out and fall asleep. And because they're alone, no one can help them. So within a couple minutes, they die—many times, unintentionally. Often it's an unintentional suicide."

He continued, "When you have time, check to see if there was a suicide note. Look for any evidence as to whether or not this was intentional. Find out what he did this evening. Talk to his friends. Retrace his steps."

Well, right now I was standing in the very last place Marky was on this earth. I was definitely going to retrace his steps, and I was starting here at the spot where he had taken his last breath only a few short hours ago. I wanted answers, and I wanted them now! I cried out to God again: "Lord, please help me! I need to know details. I want to see where Marky died. I want to sit where he sat. I want to know what he was thinking and feeling, Lord. Please, please, please, I have to understand why."

I'm sure the concrete floor of the pavilion was splattered with tears as I begged God to answer me. I suddenly noticed a figure standing on the hill just thirty feet away from me. As he looked down into the pavilion, he asked, "Are you the father?"

"Yes," I replied, nodding my head up and down—and well aware that God was answering my pleas.

"Do you want to know what happened?"

"Yes," I whimpered. "Please tell me."

As he walked toward me, I noticed he held a piece of rope about six feet long. When he handed it to me. I stood motionless. He was about to tell me where my son had died and what he had seen of the last scene of Marky's life on earth. It was truly by God's strength, and His strength alone, that I didn't pass out from the pain of the moment and the fear of what I was about to hear.[17]

DETAILS

"The police arrived at about 2:30 a.m., and your son's car was parked over there," he said, and he pointed to the parking lot on the west side of the park some one-hundred yards away. "The police must have noticed the car and decided to investigate since the park closes at 11. Another police cruiser soon arrived, and so did an ambulance. I live right there across the street," he explained as he pointed to his house.

"I walked over to see what was happening. I stood there on the hill where I was just standing. From there I saw your son lying on the ground right here." We walked to the spot where Marky had been lying when they tried to revive him. "He had been sitting at this picnic table, and he must have used this bar." The man pointed to one of a dozen iron crossbars that ran horizontally across the inside of the pavilion's roof. The eighty-year-old pavilion and the two-inch diameter solid-steel but rusty bars were a roof support system just ten feet off the ground—and only six feet above the twenty or so picnic tables scattered throughout the pavilion.

"The police and paramedics did everything they could do for your son. I believe he had already passed away by the time the first officer arrived on the scene."

It was later estimated that Marky had passed away at least an hour before his body was discovered. The police officer later told me that when he walked over the hill and looked down into the pavilion, it looked as if Marky were sitting at the picnic table. He still had on his ball cap, his cigarettes and lighter were sitting to his right, and his hands were resting on the table. As he pointed his flashlight toward Marky, the officer called out to him. That's when the officer saw the rope stretching down from the bar above the picnic table. Marky's body was resting six inches off the picnic bench. I later found out that the officer called for backup and rushed to Marky's aid, but it was too late.

My mind raced. *Was this intentional? Or was this an accidental suicide? I need more answers, Lord! I need to know!* I needed to trace more of Marky's steps. So I cried out to God again, "Help me, Lord!"

The man said that, in the dark, the police hadn't seen the six-foot-long rope he had handed me. Missed by the police, it had been lying some ten feet away, hidden in the grass behind the trunk of Marky's car. It was later determined that Marky must have cut the rope at his trunk and thrown the remaining six-foot piece into the grass....

The gracious man could give me no more information. He offered his condolences, shook my hand, and said good-bye... and I was alone.

I later became friends with this man—Dave—whom God sent into my life that early morning in response to my cries for answers. Dave is a true friend who will always have a special place in my heart. Of course we share the bond forged that early morning in Edgewood Park, but our bond became stronger and eternal when, four years after Marky's death, Dave asked Christ into his heart at the very same park.

So now I knew where my son had sat and where he had breathed his last breath. I noticed three fresh cigarette butts—his brand—on the concrete floor next to the table. Marky had sat there feeling—the Lord revealed to me—scared and afraid, alone, and acting out in a desperate cry for help. I was sure that the spiritual warfare had raged intensely as Satan tried to convince him that he would be better off dead, but why would Marky do this? In my heart of hearts—deep down inside—I knew Marky's suicide was unintentional, but at the moment everything suggested that he had succeeded at what he had set out to do. I wasn't sure...

It was now between 7 and 8 a.m. on July 12, 2005, some six hours after I had received Carly's frightening and nightmarish phone call. As I sat at Marky's picnic table, in the same spot he had sat under that wretched bar, I quickly thought back over the past several days with Marky. I wanted to figure out what events might have led to this tragedy. I remembered a similar tragic event happening in that same pavilion just a couple years earlier: another young man had died the same way Marky had...

I continued seeking God, crying out to Him relentlessly for answers.... and He answered again, again, and again.

6

To Comfort Those Who Mourn

As I sat alone at the picnic table crying so hard I was barely able to breathe, the enemy was very much at work—feeding on my pain, my heartache, and, consequently, my irrational thoughts. I wanted one thing and one thing only: I wanted to die. I didn't want to live out this nightmare; I didn't want to feel this pain anymore. My flesh—overwhelmed and reeling from heartache and shock—was at war with my spirit. God was calling me to trust Him to help me survive, one attack at a time, this vicious assault by the enemy of my soul. The battle raged![18]

THE LIE FROM THE PIT OF HELL

As I sat at that table in the pavilion, I thought, *I can end my life right here, right now.* I had a rope. I could do it, and my pain would end. *And I would be with Marky.*

As always, Satan attacked the mind, and I entertained the thoughts he planted. I was literally just seconds away from being in heaven… from being with Marky. The pain was so intense, so real, so physical, and so potentially deadly.

And the lie was so easy to believe. *I can't live through this*, I thought. *It is unbearable.*

But God intervened through His Holy Spirit within me. *What about Carly, Juliana, Brooke, and Dominic? Your other children need you. It would be wrong to put them through your death as well as Marky's. I am your Strength. I will be your Strength.*

At that moment I knew, deep within, that I had to live by the Spirit. I could not let what I was feeling in my mind and body guide my steps.

FLESH OR SPIRIT?

As intense as this struggle within me was, the real battle was raging in the heavenly realms. I knew that Satan was trying to kill me, that he was sending my way all the demons I had been delivered from since I'd accepted Jesus as my Savior. I was the target of an all-out assault. My son was gone from this earth, and now the demons wanted me dead too. And they wouldn't stop there, I was sure. My wife, my other children, my family, my friends, Marky's friends—they would also be the focus of this all-out assault as Satan tried to stop what God good planned to do in our lives. The enemy's passion is always to prevent whatever God wants to do in us and through us, His children. I felt too weak to even put on my spiritual armor, too weak to pray as I wanted to pray. But God was my strength, and I am confident that—as promised—the Holy Spirit interceded for me when I couldn't pray for myself (Romans 8:26). And by God's grace, I didn't succumb to the enemy's attack. The rope rested in my hands...

Sitting alone at the picnic table, I kept crying. I desperately wanted and needed more answers from God—and He answered yet again....

I remembered the other young person who had died in the pavilion two years prior. He had also hanged himself. As I looked up at those hideous bars all across the underside of the roof, I decided that no one else would ever again be able to do what Marky had done. I had a mission: *This pavilion has to come down, and I'm the one to make that happen!* A rage consumed me, and I felt myself filled with a fiery hatred of this awful place. I hated the fact that two beloved children had died here. I hated because my flesh was overwhelming my spirit. I was a seriously hurt and deeply wounded child of God, enraged by my pain almost to the point of being out of control. *Satan was not going to kill another child. Not here—not ever again—not in this way!*

Walking to my car, I planned how I would demolish that horrible place. "No more!" I cried. "Never, never again!" I raced back toward my house to get money to buy a saw: I was going to cut those bars and level that pavilion!

Only by God's grace did I make it safely back to my home some twenty minutes away. When I entered the house, I could see the fear and concern on my wife's face. "Are you all right? What happened?" she asked, also searching for answers. Our three younger children were still asleep, still unaware of their big brother's death.

"I'm going to tear that place down!" I raged. "This is the second death there, and there will be no more!" I grabbed my wallet and hurried out the door. Now I was utterly out of control.

But God got my attention a moment later....

GETTING MY ATTENTION

I flew down the highway entrance ramp at what must have been 80 or 90 mph when I suddenly had to slam on my brakes to keep from hitting a slower moving car several hundred yards ahead of me—and I stopped literally inches from the rear bumper. Numb and in shock, I read the car's license plate: ISAIAH 61. No specific verse or phrase came to mind when I read that reference, but I knew that God had wanted me to see it. I knew that He wanted me back walking with Him in the Spirit, not being controlled by my pain-filled flesh.

What was the message behind the license plate? Here are the first three verses from Isaiah 61:

> *The Spirit of the Lord God is upon Me,*
> *Because the Lord has anointed Me*
> *To preach good tidings to the poor;*
> *He has sent Me to heal the brokenhearted,*
> *To proclaim liberty to the captives,*
> *And the opening of the prison to those who are bound;*
> *To proclaim the acceptable year of the Lord,*
> *And the day of vengeance of our God;*
> *To comfort all who mourn,*
> *To console those who mourn in Zion,*
> *To give them beauty for ashes,*
> *The oil of joy for mourning,*
> *The garment of praise for the spirit of heaviness;*
> *That they may be called trees of righteousness,*
> *The planting of the LORD, that He may be glorified.*
> ISAIAH 61:1-3

God plans our days and choreographs our appointments, and even in my pain I knew that this slow-moving car was a wakeup call for me.

Isaiah 61 continues to serve as a purpose statement for our ministry to this day: We exist "to heal the brokenhearted . . . to console those who mourn . . . to give them beauty for ashes and the oil of joy for mourning." (You can read all of Isaiah 61 in appendix E, section 9.)

I know of no worse pain and broken-heartedness than what comes with the death of a child. Sadly, millions of hurting parents think they will never see their child again, but they can find hope in Jesus Christ. When they choose Jesus Christ as their Savior and Lord, they can be confident that they will once again see their child and that they will share eternity together. That is the foundation of our hope and the heart of our healing message.

A WICKED METAL SNAKE

I took a deep breath... and then hurried off to the hardware store to buy a saw to remove those wretched bars.

When I arrived back at the park, several of Marky's friends were there. I slowly climbed up on Marky's picnic table where my precious son had first fallen asleep and then breathed his last breath.

I attempted to cut through the bar that Marky had used. *This one, this bar, would be first to come down,* I thought. *No one else's children will ever, ever use this bar to hurt themselves in this tragic way. Enough is enough!*

Thinking that the metal bars would be hollow, I had bought a hacksaw at the store. But these bars were eighty-year-old, two-inch-thick, solid steel bars, and this little saw was absolutely no match for them. I would have been there for days—especially if I were to take down all twenty-three of the twenty-foot-long bars. Two cuts each... Forty-six cuts... *I need an electric Sawzall,* I thought. *That can cut through anything.* I questioned the kids who were gathered near the pavilion—Did they live nearby? Did anyone own a Sawzall?—but no one knew anything about that tool.

Then I remembered that my cousin Don owned a Sawzall, and he lived only a few miles away. As I raced to his house, I called him to tell him the news about Marky. He was in shock, but he said he wanted to go back to the park with me. Don had known and loved Marky, too, and he was very aware of how much I loved my son and how close we had been. Don could not imagine the pain I was in, but he didn't want me to be alone in it.

When we arrived at Edgewood, Don knew me well enough not to try to persuade me to stop this. I plugged in the extension cord and began to cut that wretched, ugly bar. It was a hugely significant act: this was my starting point for dealing with this immense pain. That bar represented everything evil to me.

This wicked and horrible place, I thought as I sawed. *This is where my son died so tragically. This place, this horrible, wicked place.* I cried as I tried to kill this awful inner pain one bar at a time.

As I grabbed the outside of the bar, the rusty casing crumbled in my hand. I grabbed on even tighter and pulled the trigger on the saw. The moment was surreal. One second I was standing on the golf course with my son; the next second I was standing on top of a table in a park trying to cut away the worst nightmare of my life. I believed I could make that nightmare disappear by removing everything that was a part of this horrible, inescapable tragedy. The thoughts kept coming into my mind—thoughts from the enemy for sure—*I will never, ever see or hold my son again—never…. I will never kiss or hug my Marky again—never…. I will never again hear him say, "I love you, Dad." Why go on living?*

I know now that this train of thought was straight from the pit of hell. And I know now more than ever that this was spiritual warfare. I had read about it, talked about it, heard others talk and preach about it, but now I myself was in the middle of the war. I was on the front lines in a battle for my family's lives and for souls that God planned to save as a result of this tragedy. I understand all this now, but at the time, those steel bars—those wretched, deadly, evil bars—were my only focus.

I quickly climbed on top of the same picnic table where my son had sat, and it took me ten long minutes to cut through one end of the bar. When I finally got through that end, the bar snapped downward, jerking up and down, back and forth, and almost knocking me off the picnic table. Since that bar was still firmly in place on the other end, I hurried to that end, climbed atop another table, and began to saw. The bars were held in place by six-inch-square end caps that went into the pavilion's one-foot-square wood beams that the roof rested upon. When I had cut through this second end, the fifteen-foot bar came crashing down, bouncing to and fro, repeatedly hitting the concrete with a loud bang and another bang, and looking eerily like a wicked metal snake. And that steel creature would never hurt a child again.

Cutting down that bar was a victory for me, a victory over something that represented total evil at that moment. Yes, I was filled with anger.

Righteous anger, I thought somewhere deep in the back of my pain-filled mind, and I believed that God was answering my silent cries for help and that angels interceded on my behalf in the heavenlies.

It felt good to yank the end caps out of the pavilion's beams. The bar was now down. Exhausted, I realized that the other twenty-two bars would have to come down another day, another way. Besides, I learned from the kids that someone had called the police and a patrol car was on its way. I didn't care. I was too busy trying to figure out a way to have someone's bulldozer complete my mission.

As I bent down and grabbed the bar, I threw it off to the side of the pavilion on the ground. "No one will ever again use that bar to die!" I said. I kept the end caps and tossed them onto the floor of the van next to the rope the neighbor had given me. I drove Don home. As he got out of the car, he said, "Let me take the rope and end caps."

"No!"

"Then please promise me you won't do anything stupid." I'm sure in our drive to and from the park I had more than once said I wanted to die. That was the way I would have dealt with my pain, but God had a different plan. His way would prove very different from mine.

7

Fleeing the Park and Death

As I drove away from Don's house, I kept looking at the rope and the metal end caps. With the pain and heartache increasing to a truly unbearable point, I was frantic for a way to escape it. When I approached a stop sign, I looked to my left and saw a pond some fifty yards from the road. I looked back at the rope and the metal caps. *I could tie that rope around the metal end caps, attach it to my legs, go into the pond, and in seconds be with my son. No more pain. No more suffering.*

I sat at the stop sign and, through my tears, looked at the rope, the metal caps, and the pond... for a long time.

"God, help me! Please help me. I can't live with this pain."

"I am your strength," I heard. With that, I drove away from the pond as fast as I could. I pressed the gas pedal to the floor until, after driving just a few hundred feet, I almost ran full-speed into a fifty-ton trash truck that had stopped dead in the road. I screeched to a halt and began to sob even harder. My heart was racing. "I am out of control, God. Help me!"

"Throw that garbage away," I heard Him say.

I quickly got out of the van, grabbed the rope and the end caps, and, as I ran to the back of the garbage truck, told the worker, "I have some trash I have to throw away!" In one motion, I tossed that garbage into the back of the truck (2 Corinthians 10:3-5).

DRIVING TO MY PARENTS' HOME

My sister, Chic, had gone to my parents' house and told them and my oldest brother, Alan, the bad news. Marky had regularly stayed with my parents for several reasons. One reason was his desire to stay in the same school district for his senior year and his last high-school baseball season. Another reason involved behavioral and anger issues that had greatly increased over the previous two years (I'll discuss these later in the book). For those two years, Marky was unable to get along with his mother and stepfather in their home. He had difficulty abiding by their rules and, for that matter, he had difficulty abiding by the rules of my home as well. Since our divorce some thirteen years earlier, I had enjoyed a very flexible joint-parenting and visitation schedule that had allowed me to have Marky and Carly half of the time. But as their teen-age years progressed, like most children of divorce, they—and especially Marky—gravitated to the home and path of least resistance. That meant living with my folks, and he did really well with my mom and dad.

Marky was dealing with some emotional issues, and this struggle was compounded during his last six months of life because, unbeknownst to us, he was dabbling with prescription medications he bought from friends and on the streets. I discovered this fact in those first three sur-real days after Marky was gone. I learned about his drug use while I was investigating the issues surrounding Marky's last days and hours before his death.

I had always asked him if he did drugs or drank alcohol. He never could lie to me—for most of his eighteen years—but within the last six months of his life, he was living a lie and desperately trying to handle it on his own.

Marky's relationship with all his grandparents was as close as a re-lationship between grandparents and a grandson could be. Marky never said good-bye to any of us without a smile, a hug, a kiss, and an "I love you, Dad," "I love you, Mom," or "I love you, Grandma and Grandpa." That is one reason why losing Marky was especially hard on everyone. He loved much and was loved so much by his family, his friends, his coaches, and everyone whose life he touched. He was an amazing and caring young man. God used him mightily throughout his brief life. As I entered their home that morning, I knew my mom and dad's hearts were broken.

We cried together and comforted one another in silence. No words were needed—no words were adequate—to express our pain and sorrow at this great loss....

My mom and dad had raised four children and been blessed with eight grandchildren. Now in their early eighties, they had recently celebrated sixty-one years of marriage. And during those sixty-one years they had shared an amazing life. My father lost his right eye during World War II and is a disabled veteran. My mother joined the Women's Army Corps Services (WACS) and, as God would have it, was my father's nurse during his recovery period in Battle Creek, Michigan. He was nineteen, and she was twenty. They had lived an amazing and eventful life together—they survived the Great Depression; my father worked hard in a factory for over thirty years and served as a city councilman for almost that long; the Kent State tragedy affected them personally—but nothing they had confronted together was as shocking, tragic, or horrifying as Marky's death. I'll never forget the pain in their eyes as the tears ran down their cheeks. We hugged, we cried, and later we would talk some more.

They did tell me Marky had been at their house the night before. He had eaten two hamburgers while watching the Major League Baseball Home Run Derby with his grandpa. Soon after, he left for his mother's house near the park. When he got there, he watched more TV with Carly, his mom, and his stepfather. After Marky left his mother's house, he met up with his girlfriend Kristina and some friends.

Marky and Kristina quarreled over something minor—one of many fights teenagers experience and definitely nothing out of the ordinary—so some friends drove Kristina home. An upset and angry Marky left separately in his car.

THE PHONE CALL

It had been a rough weekend for Marky, starting Friday afternoon—three days before his passing—when I was with him and my two cousins at Brookside Country Club....

We had an early tee time, and when it was Marky's turn, I looked at him with a peace and a joy unlike anything I had ever felt before. I was so proud of him. He had just completed his senior year at Barberton High School and, during baseball season, starred at second base.

A feeling of gratitude began to well up in my heart as each hour passed. I could not thank God enough for Marky as well as my four other children and my wife. I thanked God and praised Him silently as the day unfolded.

Looking back, I see that God was preparing my heart for the life-changing experience of Marky's sudden passing, yet of knowing the Lord's tremendous grace and mercy in new ways, and I responded with praise and thanks. God knew exactly what the following week had in store for me, and He gave me this extraordinary time with Marky. God knew my heart was right as I gratefully thanked Him all day long for the precious gifts in my life: my family, my children, my son.

We were on the seventeenth green in the early afternoon when Marky's phone rang. A look of horror came across his face as he listened to the caller.

"No, no, no . . . Oh, man... Oh, man…. What happened?"

A friend on the other end of the line was telling Marky that their friend Christina—not Marky's girlfriend, Kristina—had hanged herself the night before. Tears fell from Marky's eyes as he turned off his cell phone and walked away from us to deal with his pain.

When I walked up to him, he told me what happened. I hugged him and told him how sorry I was.

"Why, Dad? Why?" he asked in confusion. Not able to answer that question, I walked away to give Marky time alone with his thoughts, with his feelings, with God. I also prayed silently for the young girl's family. And I remember thinking, *I am so glad it wasn't one of mine.* At that moment, as selfish as it sounds, I felt even more grateful for my children.

When I said good-bye to Marky in the parking lot a few minutes later, he was still upset. I tried to console him as he repeatedly looked to me with bloodshot, teary eyes for an answer.

"What was she thinking, Dad? Why would she do that?"

Trying to console him, I hastily answered, "She wasn't, Marky. She wasn't thinking. Promise me, son, that you will never do such a thing— no matter what—no matter how bad . . ."

He interrupted me. "Oh, Dad, I could never—I would never . . ."

We hugged and I kissed him good-bye. He assured me he was all right, but the spiritual warfare had begun—and I didn't realize that fact until it was much too late.

"WHAT WAS SHE THINKING?"

When I was retracing the days and hours before Marky's death, his friends told me that he kept asking, "Why would she do that? Why would someone do that to her friends and her family?" In front of several people after Christina's funeral services, Marky even said, "I could never do that to my dad or to Dominic." Dominic was his then-five-year-old brother who idolized him. "It would kill them." Thinking back on this statement confused me greatly....

Marky was the type of person who would do all he could to figure out what another person was thinking. He would try to stand in that person's shoes in order to understand what thoughts were guiding his or her actions. I could easily imagine this quest for understanding prompting Marky to get close to Christina's frame of mind by placing a rope around his neck. He wouldn't have known that in two or three seconds, as the medical examiner had explained, he would pass out. This explanation of Marky's death made more sense to me than anything else so far.

And this explanation was supported by the discovery that the rope had never been tied around the bar. According to the police on the scene, the rope had only looped around the bar three or four times. Wouldn't Marky have tied a knot if he had wanted to die? I needed more answers, and God would soon provide them.

I felt I found one important answer in the rust that crumbled into my hand when I touched that old metal bar. The soft cotton rope must have gotten caught in all the rust. So when he sat down, Marky must have believed that the rope would unravel. Instead, it had tightened against the rust, and he had passed out. I was convinced he was trying to understand his friend's thinking. Then in an instant he was asleep and escorted into heaven by angels.

To this day, I believe in my heart that this explanation is accurate and true: Marky made a mistake. He messed up. But he didn't mean to take his own life. Of course only God knows for sure; on this side of heaven I will never know for certain. Whether Marky's suicide was intentional, unintentional, or a matter of his simply, but fatally getting too close to death in an effort to understand Christina or alleviate his pain—some things only God Himself knows (Isaiah 55:8-9, Psalm 39:4-5 NLT).

TREASURES IN HEAVEN

God knew the day Marky and you and I would be born, and only He knows the exact day and hour you and I will die. I hold fast to the truth that only God controls both the starting point and the endpoint of a person's life on this earth. The Lord knows all: the day, the hour, and the moment of our birth as well as the day, the hour, and moment of our earthly departure. Who am I to question His sovereign right to that knowledge?

> *I do know that those of us who believe that Jesus is God's perfect*
> *Son, sent to earth to take on the punishment for our sins, have*
> *treasures awaiting us in heaven.*
>
> *Do not store up for yourselves treasures on earth, where moth and*
> *rust destroy, and where thieves break in and steal. But store up*
> *for yourselves treasures in heaven, where moth and rust do not*
> *destroy, and where thieves do not break in and steal. For where*
> *your treasure is, there your heart will be also.*
>
> MATTHEW 6:19-21 NIV

And I know now that after I kneel in gratitude, face-to-face with my Lord and Savior Jesus Christ, I will then run to one very special treasure: my son who awaits me in heaven. I can still hear Marky's words from that beautiful day in October 2000: "Daddy, I'm ready to accept Jesus as my Savior." Those words give me total peace and confidence that one day we will be together again.

The greatest gift we can receive and share with our families and friends is salvation in Jesus Christ. At the very moment the people we love receive Jesus Christ into their heart, into their lives, they receive the gift of eternal life in heaven. Then, upon their death, they go immediately from life on earth to life in heaven. Ultimately, all things on this earth will pass away, but our salvation in Jesus Christ is a promise that lasts forever and ever throughout eternity.

8

Telling Marky's Siblings

In the early afternoon, I made the twenty-minute drive back home. Dena and I needed to tell Juliana, then age 12, Brooke, 10, and Dominic, 5, that their big brother was no longer here, but was now in heaven. Each had loved their older brother so much, and Dena had watched her stepson grow from an energetic five-year-old into a godly young man. The pain was beyond words.

As I drove along, I asked God what to do. I needed to know from Him how to properly explain this difficult situation to our children. I knew that wherever we were when they heard the horrible news, they would always remember that place. So I didn't want to tell them in our home or anywhere we would ever visit again. This wisdom was supplied by the Lord.

I called my wife from the car, and she agreed that we would drive somewhere to tell the children. When the five of us were in the car, it was eerily quiet. As the kids sat in silence, I could tell they sensed something was wrong.

"YOUR BROTHER IS IN HEAVEN"

We drove to a park in a neighborhood we had never visited—and would never visit again. As we got out of the car, I asked the children to gather on the small deck of the cottage that overlooked this serene and picturesque setting. Then I silently asked God to give me words that would ease the children's pain. Then, gently, quietly, I said, "Marky passed away today, and he is now in heaven."

All five of us began to cry, and Dena and I tried to embrace the children to give them comfort. Juliana and Brooke wept inconsolably, and Dominic slowly walked away from us, leaned against a wall, and whimpered pathetically as huge tears rolled down his cheeks. "Marky's in heaven," I told him. "He's okay."

"I miss Marky!" he cried out. "I want Marky!"

"I do too, son. I do too." And I bent down to hold him.

After several minutes I noticed a man fishing at the pond, and I broke the tension by asking the kids to walk to the pond. The man was gracious enough to let us use a pole, so Dominic, Brooke, and I fished for ten or fifteen minutes. It was as if my life were moving in slow motion; I felt numb mentally and emotionally.

Physically, though, I felt tired and sick to the core inside. *Will this pain ever go away?* I hurt in ways I had never hurt before, but deep inside I had to be—I wanted to be—strong for my family. *They will go as I go, so I must be strong for them.*

As we drove back home, the children were once again quiet, and their silence was deafening. We were a severely broken family, and the wound of losing Marky had resulted in shock and pain beyond imagining. Each waking moment felt like a nightmare, and I just wanted to this horrific dream to end.[19]

LOOKING BACK

I can look back now, some four years after Marky's passing, and see why the warfare was so intense. Already in this relatively short span of time, a multitude of people have heard my testimony that God answers a father's cries. God has used this true story to bring thousands of souls to salvation, and millions of people have been reminded of how precious God's gift of life is and have heard a message about the hope and healing available to us through Jesus Christ. As the spiritual battle raged over the next several days, many souls were at stake. God knew that fact. Satan knew it as well. I simply wanted the searing pain to go away.

And maybe you know the feeling. Maybe you've walked this path or a similar one. Perhaps, like me, you've entered a season of life so unexpectedly—you were entirely unprepared and, as a result, so utterly confused—it literally knocked not only the breath out of you but also every ounce of energy, hope, and even the will to breathe or live.

What had been reasons for concern and worry last week paled against this sudden turn of events. After all, your life as you knew it was over. What was your reality no longer is your reality. Whatever you dreamed, you no longer dream. Whatever you hoped to experience in your future is no more. Life seems over. Finished. Done.

THE CRIES OF A FATHER

When we feel pain, hurt, anger, loss, or shock beyond anything we could ever have imagined, we who name Jesus as our Savior and Lord choose to remind ourselves that God is God and that, for those of us who love God, all things work together for good—for the good of our becoming more like Christ. Father God loves us, and He showed us this love when He gave His only begotten Son Jesus to take on the punishment for all our sins by dying on the cross. Yet Jesus overcame that death and the sin that prompted it: He rose from the dead to give us life—life abundant on this earth and life eternal in heaven.

God grieves for all of His children on this earth who die each day without ever acknowledging His awesome gift of love on their behalf. We can never imagine the pain He must feel over souls lost to hell for eternity. The pain, heartache, and anxiety we feel on this earth—as intense as those emotions can be—are nothing next to the pain God feels as a result of His children willfully rejecting Him, dying without ever having known Him or loved Him, dying and now required to spend eternity apart from Him.

NOTHING BETWEEN YOU AND GOD

Why does it often take a tragic loss or a valley-of-death experience for us to turn to God? I will tell you why. I am a father who, at the loss of my son, needed God so desperately that I was unable to utter a word. I needed God for every breath I could take. I depended upon God for the very will and the ability to move forward just one more step. The shock and pain were so intense that death looked like the only escape from the throbbing heartache. Even simple aspects of living—breathing, eating, walking, talking—were now major challenges.

When you find yourself in this kind of a physical, emotional, and spiritual state, you realize that nothing stands between you and God. You stand alone with your faith—whatever or whomever you have placed your faith in. You stand alone on whatever beliefs you have accepted as true. You stand alone before your Creator—if, by His grace, you are able to recognize that fact. If you choose to turn to God, you will see that He is waiting to receive you.

Some hurting people, however, choose alcohol, drugs, their mates, or their fix of choice—and whatever they choose will not help. I cannot imagine going through this horrible nightmare—this tragic loss of Marky—without God walking before me and beside me each step of the way. I would have been dead years ago, either by my own hand or slowly with drugs and alcohol. I totally understand why other children die, why marriages fall apart, and why people are eaten alive by their pain: as Satan has his way again and again, tragedy leads to more tragedy.

When we are in the valley—taken there by pain or loss beyond description—we aren't worried about the bills that need to be paid, the possible real estate sale, the grass that needs mowing, or the game the baseball team should have won. Such matters are totally unimportant, because you may soon find yourself battling in that valley for your life and your very soul.

Again, each one of us has a choice to make when we are in that valley: we can either seek God and turn to Him, or we can blame God and run away from Him. The choice we make is truly a matter of life or death for us and often for people we love.

TUESDAY AFTERNOON AND EVENING

I drove Dena and the children back to our home, and we spent the remainder of that first day without Marky visiting my parents and talking to his friends.

At least I had learned some answers to my questions about his last day on this earth. Marky had carried on in the most ordinary way—not like someone planning his death later that night. He'd played basketball at the park. He'd had dinner at Grandma's and watched the Major League Baseball home run derby. Then he'd visited his mother until about 11 p.m. There was a small argument with his girlfriend, and he continued to express sadness and confusion about his friend's suicide: *What was she thinking? I could never do that to my dad and Dominic. I could never do that to my family.*

Marky's words kept ringing in my mind. Over and over. And they raised in my mind the nagging question *Why, then, Lord? Why did this happen?* I firmly believed in my heart of hearts that Marky had not really intended to die.

9

The Days Before the Funeral

THE MORNING OF DAY #1

Early in the morning, in the middle of each of those first three nights after Marky passed away, the heavenly spiritual battles for my life continued to rage, and God faithfully answered my cries for help....

At exactly 3:30 each morning, I was awakened by a miraculous movement of the Lord. And He stirred not at 3:31 or 3:29, but at 3:30 sharp each of those mornings.

The first middle-of-the-night wake-up call was a song playing on television, on the Christian music station I had left on to help me fall asleep. I woke rather suddenly to the lyrics of "You" by The Afters. The abruptness of my waking made me wonder if everything I had experienced had been a dream, a nightmare. I lay in bed and scrambled to clear my mind. *Was this all a dream or was my son really dead?* The words of the song broke through my confusion.

Lying there in bed, I gasped for breath as tears flowed from the corners of my eyes, rolled down my cheeks, and ran down the back of my neck, settling on the pillow beneath my head. I cried as I realized that Marky really was gone, and I quietly listened to the words of the song:

You

My heart is as frail as a dove
And my spirit is as weak as a rose

See my sorrow, feel my pain
You're my refuge, You're my reason,
My strength in this beautiful place
That's where I find God

You're in my heart, You're in my soul
You are my heaven, You're my home
You're my best friend, You're my true love
You are my treasure, You're my God

I watch as the mountains fall down
And the rivers part at Your feet
Your creation sings Your praise
Even winds obey and angels bow down
At Your beautiful voice
That's where I find God

[Repeat chorus]

You're in my heart, You're in my soul
You are my heaven, You're my home
You're my best friend, You're my true love
You are my treasure, You're my hope
You are my peace, You are my joy

You are my Savior, you are my God

A SANCTUARY, A GRIEVING PLACE, A BATTLE ZONE

Just two weeks earlier, at the end of June, God had used us to prepare a sacred place for peace and, now, for grief. Marky, his girlfriend
Kristina, Dominic, Brooke, Juliana, Dena, and I had worked vigorously
on our in-ground concrete pool and cabana house. We had drained the
pool, patched the concrete, and then freshly painted every inch to perfection—and none of us could have known that Marky was helping us
prepare a place where his own father could grieve, fight, and ultimately
be victorious in the Lord in a battle against Satan; a sanctuary where I
could safely be alone to mourn, to praise, and to worship. We had simply
thought that we were getting the pool and cabana ready for our July 4
family picnic.

My poolside sanctuary

Marky hard at work

(Top): Marky and Kristina refinishing the pool; (bottom) Many hands make light work

Our home at the time was a 160-year-old farmhouse resting on two beautiful, tree-filled acres in Bath, Ohio. The original farmhouse in the community, it sat on five hundred acres of the most pristine land in the county. The sixty-year-old concrete pool and cabana house were nestled down in a ravine some three hundred feet from the home. That pool truly was a sanctuary for me, a place of real peace, and soon it would serve as my safe place as well as the site of intense spiritual battles....

As the song finished playing, I began to cry even harder. I sat up in bed to catch my breath and realized even more fully that this was no dream. I began to weep aloud so hard that I had to leave the house so I wouldn't wake the children. Silently praying for me and desperately wanting to comfort me, Dena reached over and placed her hand on my back. *Where should I go?* I thought to myself. *Outside! Just somewhere outside* . . . I had to get out of that house.

I walked out the back door and eventually made my way down to the pool where I could grieve privately and cry aloud to God without bothering anyone.

I was in frighteningly deep pain, so, crying, I lay down, curled up in a fetal position and unable to move, right there at the side of the pool. I later learned that my cries, prompted by the excruciating pain inside, could be faintly heard at my home as they echoed in the ravine during those early morning hours.

"I CAN'T DO THIS, GOD!"

Again, lying curled up next to that beautiful refurbished pool, all I could do was cry out to God to help me make it through this living nightmare. Satan, as I mentioned earlier, is the accuser of the brethren who wages war against the saints (a New Testament word for believers) day and night (see Revelation 12:10). I clearly heard his accusations: *I should have saved my son.*

In another attack, the enemy again went straight to my father's heart: *I should have joined Marky and his friends in that pool last week at the July 4 picnic.* We had enjoyed a big gathering of family and friends for the holiday. Marky asked me to join them swimming, but, self-conscious about my weight, I was too embarrassed to take my shirt off. At the time I was about thirty pounds overweight, so I made excuses not to swim.

THE BATTLE FOR YOUR MIND

As you yourself may have experienced, one way Satan attacks our minds is by sowing such "should have" thoughts, and we make a serious mistake when we engage him by simply entertaining those ideas. This engagement is dangerous because those evil ideas can ultimately grow into major feelings of false guilt. When you suffer the death of a child, Satan continuously throws at you thoughts about you what you could have or should have done. Those flaming arrows or fiery darts can cut deep and do great harm to our soul and inner being.[20]

As the thought of not swimming with Marky consumed me—*What a wretched father I am. I should have swum with Marky. I know I let him down*—my pain intensified. In response, the enemy escalated his attack: "You can end this pain . . . right here, right now." I had opened the door of my mind just a crack, and the enemy stepped in. "End the pain. Just roll yourself into the pool. You—who should have swum with your son. You—who are such a failure as a father. You—who let him down."

But then the Holy Spirit intervened.

"IT'S NOT ABOUT THE STUFF ANYMORE"

In my spirit, I heard Marky's own voice interrupt the barrage of Satan's accusations: *It's not about the stuff anymore, Dad. It's about saving souls.* From where Marky was—and he was resting at peace in heaven—life definitely wasn't about the stuff anymore. And hearing that truth made me shake free from the enemy's claws. I was back in the moment, and I clearly knew that God would have me remember and honor my son by giving God glory while celebrating the precious gift of life. I knew with total clarity that I was to offer the hopeless and the hurting a message about the hope and love of Jesus Christ, about salvation from our sin, abundant life on earth, and eternal life in heaven. From Marky's heavenly perspective, where he was resting and at peace, life wasn't about the stuff anymore. And life is no longer about the stuff of this world to any child in heaven awaiting family members and loved ones.

And I became free of the accuser at that very moment—and I will recall that victory again and again throughout my days on this earth. This revelation gave me an anchor to hold onto; this God-given, redemptive purpose helped me survive both the 24/7 pain and the future battles against the devil's false accusations.

It wasn't easy for me to accept the painful reality that Marky was gone from this earth, but do remember that our children who have gone before us to heaven are no longer concerned about the things of this world. They want one thing and one thing only: for us to join them in the presence of the Lord where there is no more crying or pain. That is all that matters to them now, not "the stuff" of this world. In God's glorious presence, our kids are not thinking about whether or not Dad swam in the pool; they're not thinking about mistakes we made as parents. So may we who have prematurely said good-bye to our children cherish the memories of the good times we had with them and may we keep in mind the wonderful truth that our children are not only part of our past: they await us in heaven and we will share a glorious future.

KNOWING GOD'S COMFORT AND STRENGTH

As the sun slowly rose behind the trees to the east, I continued to cry out to the Lord, "I can't do this anymore!" I heard again, "I am your strength." So, taking a deep, slow breath, I rose on one knee and then on the other. And I lifted my hands to the heavens in praise. I thanked God for loving me, and I thanked Him for His precious gift of salvation in His Son Jesus… because that promise of salvation gave me the unshakable assurance that my son was in heaven. That promise was God's guarantee that I would see my son again one day.[21]

I walked over to the cabana house, turned on the CD player, and began to praise God, one song after another song after another. I lifted my face and my hands toward heaven as, for hours, I sang praises to the Lord. Then something miraculous happened: God spoke to me again, and this time I wrote and I wrote and I wrote. And on the next couple days God met me in a similar way: He was meeting me in my pain as I mourned, worshiped, and praised Him. I had never before been in such a place with the Lord. By His love, grace, and mercy, I—with a broken, humbled, and contrite spirit—had entered the throne room of the Creator of the universe. I rejoiced in His response to my cries for help. God revealed Himself to me in miraculous ways, and I still see His work in my life impacting me to this day. The message of hope He has given me has already been shared from Ohio to Florida and, through this book, has become available around the world in over one hundred countries and dozens of languages.

As I wrote, for instance, God revealed to me in those pages what I am to do for the remainder of my life. And what a source of joy that calling is! Yet sometime that morning I came across the scene from the gospels where, on the eve of His crucifixion, Jesus was in the garden praying and His disciples did not stay awake even for just one hour (see Matthew 26:38-46). I was saddened and convicted by His great disappointment in them. Crying aloud to God, I promised Him that I would finish this race and that, in His strength, I would respond to His call on my life and do everything He asked me to. I would stay awake that one hour, even if that hour were another twenty or thirty years of life on this earth. As badly as I wanted to join Marky in heaven, Satan was not going to take my life. Ever.

I chose to let God be God. "Lord," I prayed, "You and You alone will determine the day and hour I go home to heaven. Nobody else will—including me. So please tell me what to do, and I will do it. Tell me what to say, and I will say it. Tell me where to go, and I will go there."

And God answered as I wrote.

DAY #2

Wednesday afternoon was difficult because we had to go to the funeral home, discuss details of the services, and choose a casket and a burial plot. Marky's mother, his stepfather, my sister Chic, my wife Dena, and I were all in attendance at these meetings that are extremely difficult for grieving parents. We tried to comfort one another as best we could, but we could do nothing to ease the pain. Not our own pain; not anyone else's. One day I had been golfing with my son, and now, just a few days later, I was choosing a casket and a burial plot. It was a nightmarish and horrible time.

Yet our culture's funeral process exists for good reason: to offer closure to those who live on. I also knew that God was calling me to encourage hurting people (nonbelievers as well as believers), witness to the truth of the gospel, and offer them hope for eternity during these proceedings. This funeral provided a place in time where unbelievers, believers, and hurting people would all gather for answers, for closure, and, possibly, to find a glimmer of hope. There was no better opportunity than this funeral service for me to witness to the love and hope we believers have in Jesus Christ. Yet speaking at the funeral and publicly facing death's excruciating sting would definitely be a step of faith for me. People *were* watching, and many were thinking, *Where is Marky's God now? And where was his God then?*

IS SUICIDE A SIN?

Another question I knew some people were wrestling with—including my former wife—was whether suicide is a sin. Her family's religion (and my family's as well), which dated back for generations, considers suicide a mortal or deadly sin. Members of that church are taught from an early age that a person who commits that act goes straight to hell for eternity.

I knew this matter would cause Marky's mother, grandparents, and family on the other side great pain and anguish. I also knew that these wrong beliefs are not in the Bible. Like many wrongfully introduced, man-made church rules, this teaching about suicide places fear in the hearts of believers as a way to control them: "If you take your own life, you will go to hell." So now the devil was aggressively attacking Marky's loved ones on his mother's side of the family.

Consider the phone call among my former in-laws that I heard about later. Marky's uncle was talking to his older brother, who was en route from southern Ohio to join his family. Their discussion of Marky's death landed them right on false religious teaching not found in God's Word. "You know," the older brother said matter-of-factly, "Marky is in hell since he committed suicide."

Marky's uncle correctly responded to his brother, "That is simply not true. That teaching is not in the Bible. It is not biblical." Marky's uncle also told me that most of Marky's family on their side held to this wrong doctrine and that, understandably, it was causing them intense pain. Not only were they dealing with the death of a child and family member they greatly loved, but they were believing a lie straight from the pit of hell: that Marky was in hell—forever.

Again, nowhere does the Bible teach that people who take their own life can lose their salvation, especially if they are battling an illness—physical or emotional—or have suffered abuse of any kind. And the fact is that most people who take their lives are physically, emotionally, or mentally ill or have suffered one or more forms of abuse in their lifetime. Our loving God would never condemn to hell a child of His who was a born-again, professed follower of Christ. We cannot lose our salvation.

Again, whether Marky died from an intentional suicide or he simply fell asleep and died in an accidental suicide—only God Himself knows for sure. Whatever happened certainly does not negate Marky's salvation or God's promise of eternal life in heaven to him and to every other believer. When we are blindsided by a tragic death, we followers of Christ must hold onto our faith in God's faithfulness to us, our hope in His redemptive power, and our conviction that His promises are true.

> The cause of death is not the issue for God; it is the "cause of life"—the *why* you lived your life the way you did—that matters most to Him.

> After our short time on this earth, each one of us will spend an eternity somewhere. Marky's "cause of life" was Jesus Christ. So Marky lives eternally in heaven with Jesus.

> You cannot lose your salvation once you have claimed Jesus as Savior and Lord and been adopted by Father God into His family.

If we could lose our salvation—and let me say again that we *cannot* lose our salvation—this possibility would contaminate, defile, and destroy the "finished work" of Jesus Christ. If He says His work is finished—and He does—it is finished! Jesus has given us the free gift of salvation, accomplished by His shed blood, His death on the cross, and His resurrection. But each of us must choose to accept this truth and the free gift of salvation Jesus offers.

Being saved, however, does not keep us from sinning again. We all mess up and keep messing up—again and again and again. And that is exactly why we need to be saved: we are sinners. *Everyone* sins, everyone falls short of God's standards, and everyone desperately needs a Savior.

> *If we claim to be without sin, we deceive ourselves and the truth is not in us. If we confess our sins, he is faithful and just and will forgive us our sins and purify us from all unrighteousness. If we claim we have not sinned, we make him out to be a liar and his word has no place in our lives.*
> 1 JOHN 1:8-10 NIV

The good news is, we are forgiven. Our sins are not forgiven because we confess our sins. We are forgiven because of what Jesus Christ did on the cross for all of us: He paid our entire sin-debt in full—past, present, and future sin. Yes, suicide is a sin, but that sin—as with all sin—has already been forgiven in the sacrificial death of Jesus Christ Himself.

That evening I shared with the entire family this message and these truths from God's Word, along with a handful of other Bible promises. Each person there, including Mike's older brother who had been so misled, was released from the bondage that comes with believing the enemy's lies.

Now don't get me wrong. Suicide is a wrong choice. It is never a solution for life's problems, and in every case it is a cry for help for a mental or emotional illness, addiction, past abuse, or other complications in life. Without question, suicide is the result of spiritual warfare, and it leaves the victim's loved ones and friends in deep, deep pain. If you or anyone you know is suicidal, I beg you to tell someone. Tell a friend, your parents, a teacher, or your pastor, or turn to one of the resources at the back of this book. Please seek help immediately.

And let me remind you that God—for whom nothing is impossible—has a plan for your life, a plan for good and not for evil!

SUICIDE AND THE CHURCH

The Hope of Survivors (www.TheHopeofSurvivors.com), one of the ministries I actively support is helping survivors of clergy sexual abuse (CSA).

One time when I was helping a man who, as a child, had been sodomized by a priest, God revealed to me the truth about suicide and prompted me to offer a series of questions for the upcoming deposition of a Cleveland (Ohio) bishop during a civil trial. This bishop was proven responsible for transferring this victim's pedophile priest from church to church, thereby giving him opportunity to further sexually assault and severely harm many more children.

The questioning followed this pattern:

"Is it true the church believes that if you commit suicide, you go to hell?"

The bishop's answer would be "Yes, according to church doctrine."

"And is it true that across this country hundreds, if not thousands, of sexually abused children have committed suicide as a result of clergy sexual abuse they received at the hands of these criminal, pedophile priests?"

One documented church case in the Midwest reported that five of fourteen altar boys sexually abused by their priest grew into adulthood and later killed themselves to alleviate the pain and mental anguish resulting from those childhood attacks.

"So then, according to the church's own doctrine, is it reasonable to assume that these same raped and sexually abused children who committed suicide are now in hell?"

The bishop would be bound by church doctrine to say yes.

"So, in conclusion, if the church's position on suicide is true, these criminally abusive priests, along with the church leaders like you who were in collusion with them, are responsible for sending these victims of clergy sexual abuse to hell."

THEY ARE NOT IN HELL

This man-made teaching about suicide victims going straight to hell is a lie. The bottom line for me is this: If the teaching is in the Bible, it is true; if the teaching is not in the Bible, then it is merely the opinion of man.

The revelation that suicide victims are not in hell has freed families across the country from the enemy's cruel deception. And I spent a major part of my initial three days of grieving dispelling nonbiblical beliefs about the afterlife that were rooted false man-made religious teaching. I assured people that Marky was in heaven because he had locked his name into the Lamb's Book of Life when he came to me that October day in 2000 and accepted Jesus as his Lord and Savior.

The Bible clearly states that we are all sinners who fall short of God's glory. [22] All of us are sinful in nature before salvation, and all of us will make mistakes and sin after salvation. However, we should sin less as we become more knowledgeable of God's Word, as we trust and abide in Christ, and as, growing in spirit and in truth, we become more like Him. We must keep our eyes fixed on God, not on our pain or our problems. When we do so, our lives will inevitably change for the better.

We are also to live in gratitude for all God has done through His Son Jesus Christ who gave His life for us. Neither His forgiveness nor the eternal life in heaven He has guaranteed us gives us the freedom to willfully sin. Instead, we believers should be motivated by love to be God's light in a very dark world.

So, yes, Marky sinned... as we all do. Marky made mistakes... as we all do. Marky got dangerously close to some things he should not have... and many of us do that too. But Marky—and we who have named Jesus our Lord—will not go to hell as a consequence for any failure or mistake.

No religion or denomination can ever take away what genuine, biblical Christianity is based upon: Jesus Christ willingly died on the cross, giving Himself as the ultimate sacrifice for the sins of all humanity. If you accept Jesus Christ as Lord and Savior of your life, you are saved. You have no hoops to jump through and no man-made rules to follow. Jesus—and Jesus alone—is all we need to be saved from the eternal consequences of our sin. Jesus Christ is the Way, the Truth, and the Life (John 14:6). On the cross Jesus said: "It is finished." There is nothing we can add to or take away from our salvation. Jesus did it all for us. We can do no work to make our salvation better, and we can make no mistake that would cause us to forfeit that salvation. The finished work of Jesus Christ is the freedom, hope, healing, and truth we can believe wholeheartedly, trust completely, and walk in every minute of every day.

Put differently, it has been said that no religion can get you into heaven and no sin can keep you out of heaven. The only unpardonable sin is this: upon your death, you have willingly, permanently, consciously, and openly denied and rejected Jesus Christ as your Lord and Savior. God will not and cannot pardon that sin.[23]

So surely Marky was not condemned to an eternity of separation from God for sinning or experiencing a moment of illness, confusion, or weakness. Such dire consequences were prevented by Jesus' death on the cross. When sinless Jesus took on the sin debt of the world, He took care of sin past, present, and future. Future sin? Yes, *future* sin—your sin, my sin, and the sin of everyone born after Jesus' death, burial, and resurrection over two thousand years ago. Jesus gave His life so that we can live forgiven for our sins and saved from the consequences of that sin, so that we can have life more abundantly.

When religion—or when man speaking with supposed religious authority—starts heaping heavy, impossible-to-carry burdens on people and requires them to live in perfection to make it safely to heaven, these false teachers have totally missed the point of God's grace and mercy evident in the shed blood of His Son Jesus. It is not by works, but by God's grace and mercy that we are saved from the consequences of our sin. If we had to be sinless after salvation, not one of us—not a single one of us—would make it into heaven.[24]

Marky was in heaven, and all the family was now at peace with that truth.

DAY #2: NEARING AN END

Wednesday was winding down, so I traveled from my former in-laws' home back to my parents' home. Making the funeral arrangements and dispelling hundreds of years of old false religious teaching had taken its toll on me emotionally and physically. I was tired and hurting. I was the encourager who needed encouragement myself. There was no better source of comfort my mother's arms. After spending some time with my folks, I then journeyed back home for some precious time with my wife and children.

I went to bed that evening exhausted. At 3:30 a.m., like clockwork, I awoke to the loudest *Boom, boom, boom!* I'd ever heard. The sound of a big bass drum echoed throughout our 160-year-old home. I lay still and I heard it again. *Boom, boom, boom!* it beat loudly.

To this day we have not been able to explain the sound. I believe it was the Lord and His angels waking me for the second night in a row to go down to the swimming pool—my sanctuary—to be ministered to again. And I obeyed. (Later that day I asked if anyone else had heard the loud drumbeat, and only my daughter Brooke had.)

Just as I had the previous night, I put on Marky's baseball cap, jersey, and batting gloves and took his baseball bat, a camera, my Bible, and my Bible on CD with me. I have some amazing photos of God's beautiful creation from this poolside sanctuary, the site of some significant steps on my healing journey.

Taking items that had been Marky's was like putting on my body armor. The act itself helped me enter into praise and worship of God. Besides, I was preparing for battle.

GOD WILL SUSTAIN US

This divine appointment started out exactly as the previous night's had. I made my way to the pool where once again I let everything out of me at once. The cries, the moans, the groans were intense, and they came from deep inside. But when I was in this sanctuary, I no longer had to be the strong husband or the strong father. I could let out my emotion—and I did. The enemy tried to come at me again just as intensely as he had the night before, but I was gaining strength. I had the Omnipotent Creator of the universe on my side, and nothing compares to His power and might.[25]

I recalled the previous night's victories and my newfound mission:

"Life is not about the stuff anymore. My life is about saving souls." I recalled the messages God had given me in the coroner's building, and I thanked Him again for the great gift of life He had given me in saving Marky at his birth. Marky was at peace in heaven. He was saved.

Still, the emotions were powerful, and I battled with them. In deep mourning, I lay by the pool in the fetal position for hours, until the sun came up. Again, I arose to one knee and then another. Before I knew it, I was again praising God as I had never praised Him before. Again there was music. I studied Isaiah 61, and I listened to the Bible on CD as I worshiped God. As God continued to answer prayers, I continued to write.

I also knew I was gaining strength from God's Word. As I mourned, I used that sword in the battle for my mind, and I spent time in praise and worship throughout the remainder of the morning. After all, "God inhabits the praises of His people" (see Psalm 22:3). I wrote nearly one hundred pages in my journal in three days.

During these surreal and incredibly painful days, God revealed Himself to me through His Word as well as through visions, signs, and wonders. I both entertained angels and was ministered to by them: God was bringing me through an intense time of healing. I prayed for God to give me strength to complete the directives He had given me, directives I had written in that tear-stained journal. I am confident that God will continue to reveal His will as I abide in Him and obey His direction for my life until the day He takes me home. It is my vow, my covenant with Him.

My son was in heaven. I knew that to be true, and I knew he was fine. And I was encouraged by the account of King David losing his seven-day-old son yet being able to praise and worship God. Once the death was confirmed, David cleaned himself up and went to the temple to worship God. When he returned to his home, he asked his servants for food and he ate. Puzzled because David had wept and fasted while the child was still alive, the servants asked him about his behavior. I completely understood David's response: "While the child was still alive, I fasted and wept. I thought, 'Who knows? The LORD may be gracious to me and let the child live.' But now that he is dead, why should I fast? *Can I bring him back again? I will go to him, but he will not return to me*" (2 Samuel 12:22-23 NIV, emphasis mine).

King David spoke rightly when he said, "I will go to him." Our children who have departed this earth await us in heaven. In God's perfect time, we will be reunited with them.

MORNING #3

It was now late Thursday morning, and I emerged from the pool a battered, yet victorious warrior who had survived the struggle on the front lines. Again, the Lord had taken me from mourning to praise and worship, and He blessed me with messages and plans that I again documented in my journal. God was showering me with words of comfort, hope, perspective, and purpose as I praised, worshiped, and journaled in that cabana house all morning on each of those first two days. At times I couldn't keep up with the glorious messages God was revealing.

I cried out to God:

Tell me what to do, and I'll do it. Show me where to go, and I'll go there. Tell me what to say, and I'll say it.

Please, God, reveal to me Your plans—plans that will give You and Your Son Jesus all the glory as I respond to this attack on my son and my family... Reveal Your plans and I will obey.

And I cried out to Him in the confidence that all things work together for good—for the good of becoming more like Christ—for those of us who love God. I was asking and seeking God, and He was hearing and responding.

God and I were not going to let Marky die in vain, and I realized more completely than ever that Jesus was worthy of my service and my life. Humbled by pain as well as by God's amazing presence with me, I was profoundly humbled. I found myself totally dependent on the Lord for my daily survival, from one moment to the next, for every breath that I would take. I had a contrite spirit, a broken heart, and a willingness to serve my God. After all, He had revealed His love to me in my brokenness in a way far greater than I ever could have asked or imagined.[26]

I can boldly testify that God gives grace to the humble (Proverbs 3:34).

10

At the Funeral Home

I was to spend the rest of my Thursday at the funeral home for the showing. The actual church service and burial would be on Friday.

We arrived at the funeral home an hour early for the family's private viewing and some time to pray. Pastor Bob from Grace Brethren Church would share a message on Thursday, and my Pastor Mike would lead the Friday service. Marky had attended both churches, and his mother and his friends occasionally joined him at the Brethren church. Pastor Bob graciously let us use his church because of the large turnout that was expected.

Marky's body looked quite different from when I had last seen him in the coroner's building. He actually looked better in those moments I was with him immediately after his death. As I looked at him now, I felt even more strongly that the view of corpses is a morbid tradition. After all, I believe that our earthly bodies are simply a vessel to hold our soul and spirit. So that was not my son lying there; Marky was alive in heaven, living his new chapter of eternal life abundantly.[27] I went near the casket only to encourage those who were hurting.

Marky was a popular student at Barberton High School. He was kind, funny, and quick witted, and he was an amazing athlete. From the time we founded the street ministry, he passed out our T-shirts—designed by my dad, with great artwork of a Spanish mission and John 3:16 on the back—to his public-school classmates. At first, he was chided, and students made fun of him. One of his friends later told me that some had called him "Jesus Boy" and "Jesus Freak." The name-calling didn't bother Marky, and he really did love Jesus. The name-calling stopped, but Marky's love for Christ did not. During the eight years that Marky handed out those two thousand shirts, most of his friends and classmates received one or two. It was Marky's quiet way of sharing Christ....

Given who Marky was, I guess I shouldn't have been surprised that the funeral service had one of the largest turnouts in the long history of the town and funeral home. An estimated fifteen hundred to two thousand people attended both services. I spent the majority of the time being an encourager to the people who lined up in the parking lot and waited for three hours to pay their respects to Marky.

On occasion, a fellow believer would be next in line, and I could rest for a moment. That brother or sister in the Lord would encourage me, and I could hear from them much-needed words of hope. Most of the time I had the peace Jesus promised,[28] but I could tell by the looks on the visitors' faces how they were grieving and whether a person was a believer, an unbeliever, or someone not quite sure. The shock, pain, and fear of death written on the faces of the unbelievers were very intense. The vast majority of the young people as well as the adults were tearful, afraid, and in deep pain.

My daughter Carly, however, was an amazing pillar of strength as she greeted friends and classmates one at a time. She had the strength of a mature, godly woman, strength far beyond her sixteen years. I could hear her repeat the same truth over and over, and her smile was radiant as she spoke: "I will be with Marky in heaven one day. He's not here. He's alive, and he is in no more pain. I know he's with Jesus."

We were a very hurting family, but I will always remember Carly's amazing courage and the warm love she showed each and every person as that never-ending line of people passed by the casket that stood only a few feet away from my daughter. Carly's strength gave me strength.

Marky's mother struggled and experienced every level of grief imaginable. There were times, though, when she tried to laugh and when she was an encourager, but most of the time she could not speak at all.

As always, my wife, Dena, was a rock, there for me every minute of those difficult days. She has the strength of a thousand men and does not waver. As a result of her rearing and because she is her mother's daughter, Dena has faith that moves mountains.

My ten-year-old daughter, Brooke, had the hardest time at the funeral home. Unable to stand in the receiving line, she spent most of the time in the arms of her mother and grandparents. Dominic and Juliana stayed off to the side with Brooke much of the time. It was a long, arduous night.

The young people—and most of those attending were Marky's friends and peers—were the ones who most needed help and encouragement. One day their friend was here, and the next he was not. Their loss of Marky was compounded by the death of their other classmate just a few days earlier. The reality of death and the question of where they would spend eternity were staring them in the face.

By His grace, though, the Lord had prepared me to be a sanctuary and a witness for these folks. I was to be a safe place for these hurting people, a place where they could gain strength from my God-given strength. They also gained hope from my God-given hope. They were encouraged because I was encouraged by my Lord and His victory over sin and death. I laughed with them, and I cried with them, one at a time, for over three straight hours that evening.

I handed out to his twenty or so baseball buddies an action photo—that had Philippians 4:13 written on it—of Mark, Jr., hitting a baseball. I then handed out several hundred more over the next several days, and that image has come to play a big part of our ministry. Nearly ten thousand of these photos have been given away as inspirational posters, all to the glory of Christ.

The next day's services at church and then at the burial site will be the toughest, I thought. But I knew God had a plan, and I was seeking Him mightily.

"I can do all things through CHRIST who strengthens me."
Philippians 4:13

#24 Mark Canfora Jr/Spring 2003
Photo taken by Mark Canfora Sr.
ReadandBelieve.com • MarkCanfora.com •
330-865-1000

Mark Canfora
MINISTRIES

Marky connecting at the plate: the Philippians 4:13 baseball poster

11

The Battle at the Poolside Sanctuary

I awoke to the sound of thunder, and the whole house shook. Sounding like the loudest cymbals I had ever heard, the old glass panes in every window of our century home rattled violently. Then came a shimmering as each panel of glass responded to the low rolling thunder: *pssssssssssshhhhhh*, *pssssssssssshhhhhh*, *pssssssssssshhhhhh*.

During the summer in Ohio, some of the most awesome thunderstorms roll in, and it feels like the rumbling is just a few hundred feet above the ground. This evening's thunder and the consequent shaking of our home were unlike any other I had ever experienced in my forty-seven years. I looked at the clock and saw the time as clear as could be: 3:30 a.m.

For the third night in a row, God was waking me up. I knew where He was taking me, and I was ready to go. I was excited about entering into His presence. The sanctuary and sacred place awaited me, and I was eager to meet with Him.

After all, I thought I had it figured out by now. As I had the previous two days, I would experience victory in battle and hours of being in God's sweet presence even as the enemy attacked. Then suddenly I sensed that this morning would be different—and it was.

The thunder continued to rumble and pound, seemingly just a few feet above my head. I left our house and headed poolside after I gathered my gear. I had no fear: if lightning struck me, that was all right; if it didn't, that was all right too. I was in God's hands and seeking His perfect will. I was walking in the valley of the shadow of death, and I knew

I could never, ever feel more pain than I was already feeling. Death was still a welcome option, but only in God's time.

I could not leave the house until I had all my weapons of warfare: Bible? Check. CD? Check. Writing materials? Check. Camera? Check. Battle attire: hat, batting gloves, bat, jersey? Check. To this day and many times as I write, I still wear Marky's Boston Red Sox baseball cap. His baseball bat stands in the corner of my office—when Dominic isn't hitting balls with it—and the baseball batting gloves in the closet are also a gentle reminder of the victories won by God's grace at the poolside sanctuary.

As I walked confidently down the driveway, a warrior going to the front lines ready for battle, I looked up to the heavens and began praising God. At that moment I felt strength like I had never felt before.

I was strong—at least stronger than I had been the two previous mornings, or so I thought—and I was already overflowing with praise to God. Hurrying toward the gate to the pool and quickly opening it, I greatly anticipated a rich time with God before the funeral service later that morning. Now on the deck, I walked right past the spot where, on the previous two days, I had writhed in pain until the sun came up. I carried my weapons of warfare into the cabana house and continued to praise God there. Holding my journal firmly in my hand, I was prepared to receive more answers from God. I felt as if I had the battle plan all laid out before me: *Is the phase of deep grieving over? Is it all about the praise and worship now?* I felt unusually strong at that moment.

I sang, danced, and praised my gracious God until the sun came up. I wrote some more and praised Him some more. I was in a new place both emotionally and spiritually, and I was ever so grateful.

Even so, I repeated what I had done the previous two days. On both mornings, the routine had offered me a rich time of being with God, and I wasn't going to mess with the pattern. So, as I had before, I left the cabana house in the early morning and took pictures of simple things like birds, clouds, and other reflections of God's beauty that was all around me in this sanctuary. And God used these simple things to revealed awesome truths to me. (You can see these and other ministry photos, listen to of truth and comfort, watch videos, and hear messages of hope at www. IveGotHope.com. Also, twenty "Songs of Hope, Comfort, and Heaven" are listed in Appendix D.)

On the first of those mornings just after sunrise, for instance, I saw

Weapons of warfare

Reflections of God's beauty

the most beautiful butterfly I had ever seen. This black silk butterfly, with blue dots on each wing, was just sitting on the pool deck outside the cabana door. Stopping in my tracks, I sat down on the stairs and watched as this butterfly flew around the perimeter of the newly refurbished pool, my sanctuary. It flew exactly seven times around this fifty-foot-long rectangular pool, just above the deck, never cutting a corner, and always in the same direction. I counted as it flew—seven. I knew that many people believe that, in the Bible, the number seven stands for perfection, and I did not discount the significance of that or of anything else that happened whenever I was so obviously in the presence of God and His healing power.

So, during the previous two days, I had finished my time with God by running seven times around the pool, in the same direction, carrying my bat. On the final lap, I removed my gloves and jersey, jumped into the pool, and fully submerged myself: a daily washing and baptism. I would wash myself in the glory of the Lord. I would come out of the pool refreshed and ready for the day ahead of me.

NO SET PATTERN FOR GRIEF

On this particular morning, I walked out of the cabana house and was about to take some pictures, do my run, and dive into the pool. I felt that the Lord had already sufficiently prepared me to go to the funeral, now just a couple hours away. I knew the Lord wanted me to speak at the service, and I thought I was ready with a message about the celebration of life.

But God took me to another place, an oh-so-familiar place. There at the side of the pool, I fell first to my knees... and then into the fetal position. I was unable to move when grief struck me as hard as it ever had. I was desperately missing my son! Yet I heard God speak to my heart: "There is no set pattern for grieving."

I had thought the order was clear! First, I mourned, then I spent some time in praise and worship, and then I received revelations from God. And I thought that, since I had felt no desire to grieve when I arrived at the pool and since I had gone straight to worship, the deep grieving process was over. I was wrong.

I laid by that pool for what seemed hours, and the Lord ministered to me. He showed me a vision of what He meant by "It's not about the stuff anymore; it's about saving souls."

I wept as He gave me a glimpse of the church and the funeral service that would take place in just a few, short hours. I saw a packed church—standing room only—and God's children desperate to hear His Word and His truth for such a time as this. All of Marky's family members were there, all sitting quietly in their own pain and grief. His friends from the baseball team and fellow students attended. They all had one thing in common: they needed to understand why. They needed to hear about God's precious gift of life and how much He loves them.

I knew the Holy Spirit gives us the words we need when we are to speak on the Lord's behalf, but I was getting a visual along with the words. I was in awe as I listened and watched as God showed me and told me much of what I would do and say.

God's instructions for me that morning were clear. After the service opened with Steven Curtis Chapman's song "With Hope," I was to share Marky's testimony: the account of his traumatic birth, the story of his salvation on October 7, 2000, when he was born again, and then a proclamation of the reality of his eternal life in heaven that God promises us in His Word. Three gifts of life; three celebrations.

I was to offer hope in Jesus Christ because He died for us and because He is there for us and with us during times like this. He will be our strength in the pain and darkness of loss—if we let Him.

And, finally, I was to ask a question of all fathers in attendance… Then, most assuredly, I would invite those in attendance to accept God's forgiveness and salvation in Jesus. We would close with the song "Choose Life" by Big Tent Revival.

God showed me a vision of hundreds of people coming forward, some even standing in the aisles, and accepting Jesus Christ as their Lord and Savior.

"It wasn't—and isn't—about the stuff anymore. It was—and it still is—about saving souls."

Now I was ready to take on God's task for me, and the time was near.

Yes, I had not understood that there is no pattern for grief, that there is no set timeframe. But I knew clearly that there is only God and that His healing ways offer the path in which we must walk and obey. This third morning was different from the first two: I'd started with praise and worship, then received a revelation from God, did some grieving, and then was blessed with further revelation from God. I am forever learning… and, as His student and disciple, I am forever at His mercy.

After my dip into the pool, I made my way to the house, and we left for the church.

ALTAR CALL OR NOT?

Upon our arrival, I learned that a leader of the host church questioned whether it was "appropriate" for me to share a salvation message and invite attendees to accept Christ as Lord and Savior.

I'm not sure if that person thought I couldn't handle such a responsibility or, given the circumstances, I wasn't capable of dealing with the pressure and pain of it all. If I tried to do this by myself, of course, without any guidance from God or His Holy Spirit, that person would be absolutely correct. But God and His Spirit would be with me, and my Pastor Mike knew it.

So the pastors of that church asked to meet with me, Marky's mother, and Pastor Mike. When I arrived at the church, Pastor Mike quickly informed me about the issue at hand. But I had a directive from God, and Pastor Mike knew we would be moving forward with the Lord's plan.

The church parking lot was packed, and so were the pews. It was standing room only—just as the Lord had shown me.

I opened the meeting and graciously thanked the senior pastor and the associate pastor for allowing us to use their church for the service as well as for dinner for friends and family afterward. Then two points were quickly raised, one by me and the other by my pastor. First I said, "If even just one person accepts Jesus as Lord and Savior today, my son will have not died in vain, correct?" They both nodded in agreement.

Pastor Mike, who has ministered at many funerals in his twenty-plus years, had offered me his words of wisdom and encouragement just before the meeting, and now he shared them with everyone in the meeting. "If there is concern about offending people with an altar call at this service, I would ask this: How can we offend them to a worse place in hell that already awaits them?"

Asked if she agreed, Marky's mother nodded yes and wiped away her tears.

I love both of those pastors to this day, and I will be forever grateful to them and their church for their unselfish service and use of their church that day.

As we left the meeting room, the senior pastor shook my hand and looked at me with compassion. I stopped, turned to him, and again thanked him for his hospitality and his heart. I also asked him to please place three writing pads on the table in the lobby so that the new believers I was expecting to join God's family could sign in. I then told him in all seriousness, "Many people are about to accept Jesus as Lord and Savior in the service this morning."

Looking at me again with sympathetic eyes, he merely nodded his head up and down. It was as if he gave me either a look of this-poor-child-is-delusional or I-pray-his-faith-sees-him-through-this.

But unknown to him, I had just been in the presence of Almighty God, the Creator of the universe, and He had given me specific visions, signs, and directives. I had nothing to lose obeying His instructions. I had a broken heart and a contrite spirit. I was forever humbled—and remarkably at peace.

12

At the Funeral

The funeral service commenced, and "With Hope" played as people wept quietly and wiped away their tears.

The most moving time for me was when Carly spoke. She stood next to me as she faced the entire gathering. It was estimated that over six hundred people attended the church service—and probably more. There was not an empty seat in the church, and many people stood throughout the service.

Carly began to talk about her big brother as if he were alive, not dead. She talked about life as Marky's sister: the good, the bad, and the ugly. She was vibrant, bold, and strong. She was confident as she assured everyone that Marky is in heaven and that she—and all believers in Christ—would see him again one day. I was inspired and very, very proud of her.

After Carly sat down, many others shared memories of Marky and words of encouragement. Marky's mother recalled his hugs and kisses and how he was always playfully pinching her cheeks. Marky's cousin Ian remembered the days when, as kids together, he and Marky terrorized everyone with their rowdy behavior. Marky's baseball coach, Hance, gave an inspirational message of hope as he put on Marky's baseball jersey and waved him home one last time. My wife, Dena, lovingly recalled the thirteen years she had been in Marky's life, especially the "crush" he had on her in the early years, beginning when he was age five, and then shifting to Dena's sister, Donna, and, in the years that followed, any girl with blonde hair.

Then it was my turn. I walked onto the stage, and the church fell absolutely silent. As I approached the podium, I prayed silently for God's strength, and I asked the Holy Spirit to give me the words He wanted me to say.

"I stand here today with a broken heart and a contrite spirit, with a contrite heart and a broken spirit, but I have hope. I believe that Marky is not in that casket, and he is not going to be in that cemetery where we are about to go." We were behind schedule because of the testimonies, and the funeral director was obviously uneasy about how the service was unfolding.

I continued: "The cemetery can wait, and the food being prepared in the basement can also wait. This gathering is not about the cemetery, the food, or any other thing of this world. We could skip the cemetery and the food. I am not on a schedule, and neither is God. He has all the time in the world for what we are going to do here, because what I have for you, right now, is far more important than anything that is going to take place after we leave here.

"Last Friday I was golfing with my son at Brookside Country Club, and just five days later, I was picking out a casket for him. I received a phone call from my daughter, Carly, early Tuesday morning, telling me that Marky was dead. I made my way to the Summit County coroner's early that morning and had time with my son in the morgue. I asked God why Marky was gone and how my life would ever be good again. I asked God how this death could ever be a good thing. Yet I knew in my spirit that 'all things work together for good for those that love God.'

"I asked God for His help and pleaded for an answer to my cry of 'Why?' When I first arrived at the coroner's, I helped unload my son from the ambulance and then removed his body from the body bag. I laid hands on his heart and asked God to raise him, to bring him back to life. God told me that Marky was not there and that He had answered my prayer for his life the day Marky was born. God answered my cry for my son's life eighteen-and-a-half years ago, and he blessed us all with Marky. I celebrate that gift of life in Marky's birth. I celebrate Marky's salvation—his spiritual birth, when he accepted Jesus Christ as his Lord and Savior on October 7, 2000, at age fourteen. I celebrate the life Marky now has in heaven for eternity: life in heaven, promised by God and sealed by His Son Jesus Christ. I celebrate a loving God who gave us these gifts of life. I celebrate a loving God who gave us these, oh, so very precious gifts of life."

I could sense the Holy Spirit's presence, and the mood of the people changed. They no longer looked afraid, and they nodded their heads up and down. From time to time I heard words of hope like "Amen" and "Thank You, Lord." There truly was hope in the air.

"Marky is in our future. We, who believe that Jesus is God's Son and the Victor over sin and death, have hope that all of our loved ones, everyone who passed before us and knew Christ as their Savior, await us in heaven. Not just Marky, but all those who believe.

"Marky was a teenager who made mistakes, as all of us do, and no one should ever be judged on a single moment of weakness—for we are all weak at times. It is by God's mercy and grace that we can make it through difficult times.

"Marky is safely in heaven. He did not lose his salvation, and you cannot lose yours other than to flat-out deny Jesus as Lord and Savior after you have been saved. Marky loved Jesus and professed Jesus as his Savior, and Marky is saved."

TRUE MEASURES OF GOD'S LOVE

I then identified what I see as a true measure of God's love: "God gave us 6,870 precious days with Marky here on earth. And what would I give to just have one more day with Marky? What would I give? Anything, everything I own, everything I have, everything I will ever have, for just one more day, one more hour, and even one more minute to hold my Marky again! To hug him, kiss him, hold him, and hear the words 'I love you, Dad,' or to say, 'I love you, son.' I'd give $10 billion for just one more day. Yet God gave us 6,870 of those precious days. That is a loving God!

"But there is an even greater measure of God's love, and that is eternity. God promises an everlasting life in heaven with our children who have passed on before us—a life forever and ever with them in eternity. This promise is for anyone and everyone who believes that Jesus is God's Son and accepts Jesus as Lord and Savior. Our children are in our future."

A QUESTION FOR FATHERS

Then I shared what the Lord had given me to share when I dropped to my knees on the pool deck earlier that morning: "As I stand here in front of this casket that holds my son's body, I want to ask all the fathers here today a question: 'Would any one of you choose to let your son die on purpose?'"

Silence gripped the room. As I stood there looking out over the vast crowd, I made eye contact with every father I could see.

"Surely, there is one father who would let his son die on purpose," I pushed.

The believers, who were filled with the Holy Spirit, understood exactly where I was going here.

"Well, there *is* a Father who chose—on purpose—to let His Son die: God the Father!

"You see, God so loves us that He gave His one and only Son, Jesus, to be beaten, bruised, battered, crucified, and killed for you and for me, so that—with Jesus' victory over sin and death—we will not perish, but have everlasting life.

"Jesus was sinless so, by His shed blood, He paid the penalty for our sin and now offers the free gift of salvation for you and for me. Jesus rose from the dead, and He sits at the right hand of God, praying for you and me especially during times like this.

"I, like everyone who believes this truth, have hope for a glorious eternal life because this is God's promise to all of us: 'If we confess with our mouth and believe in our heart Jesus Christ is Lord we will be saved.' You are one prayer away from guaranteeing yourself a place in heaven forever.

"No, there is not a father here who would choose to let his son die. But God made that choice, and Jesus laid down His life for us—for Marky, for me, for you. And you can make a choice now. You can choose to recognize Jesus as God's Son, receive His forgiveness, and welcome Him as your Savior and Lord.

"But don't make the decision to come forward because of Marky or because of the emotions of this day. Make this decision because you know God loves you and because of what His Son Jesus did for you.

"Choose life in Christ. Choose life!"

Pastor Mike was by my side as I concluded my message, and we invited everyone who was going to choose a life in Christ to come forward.

The song "Choose Life" played, and the vision God had given me was happening before my eyes. All that He had shown me by the pool was coming true. People completely lined the altar, and the aisle filled up. Others rose to their feet, and many lifted their hands to the heavens. Marky's mother was front and center as she stood next to Carly and, by her actions, made a statement of faith in Jesus. Over three hundred people were saved that day.

The Bible says all the heavens rejoice when people are saved.[29] My son was in heaven: His friends, family members, and his mother were now saved—and that was all that matters to him or any of our loved ones who await us in heaven. Their desire is for us to, in God's time, join them one day. Again, life isn't about the stuff anymore; it's about saving souls. It's all that mattered as I spoke at Marky's memorial service, and it's all that matters now. God sent Jesus to save souls, and, with a flood of tears, I knew I wanted to be part of this salvation work of God and be His servant for the remainder of my life. Writing this book is just one of the many directives I received from the Lord in those valley days, and He honors such obedience. Miracle after miracle has occurred since Marky went to heaven to be with Jesus, and thousands of people have been saved.

CROSSING OVER FROM DEATH TO LIFE

I believe one of the greatest miracles of all is when someone accepts Jesus as Lord and Savior. When people cross over from where they are naturally—from facing eternal death and separation from God forever, to eternal life spent forever with their Creator-God—this truly is the greatest miracle of all!

As you read or listen to this book, you are part of God's answer to my cries for help, healing, and direction, to bring good out of Marky's passing. You are now a part of this move of God if, through any part of this message, you have been inspired, encouraged, or given even a ray of hope. And I pray that you have.

Nearly 3,000 attend the 2009 Celebration of Life Festival in Panama City Beach, Florida

Crossing over from death to life . . . 2007 Celebration of Life Festival, Edgewood Park, Barberton, Ohio

2008 & 2009 Celebration of Life Festivals, Edgewood Park, Barberton, Ohio

And believers were increasingly added to the Lord, multitudes of men, women and children, Acts 5:14

13

Beyond the Park

The day of the funeral service was long and grueling. Having been an encourager to others—to my family, our friends, Marky's friends, and unbelievers—I was extremely exhausted both mentally and physically. After we returned from the cemetery, we gathered at the church for the traditional after-the-funeral meal. On our way home, my wife and I decided to take our three little ones to the Putt-Putt golf course and go-cart track near our home to get their minds off all the sadness. This was an attempt to establish some normalcy for our broken and hurting family. By no means did I want to do this, but I knew I had to do this for the kids.

We were on our way home after spending several hours at the recreation center when Carly called me. She was very upset: "Daddy, a bunch of Marky's friends were in the pavilion at the park getting drunk, and I yelled at them to stop." She was angry, because just hours earlier several of them had come forward at the church and accepted Jesus as their Lord and Savior. I quickly explained that they had learned to use alcohol to deal with pain, that they will learn Jesus is their answer, but that learning that lesson will take time. Still noticeably upset, she said a few kids were still there. I offered some comfort and hung up. Within seconds the Lord spoke to me: "Go to the park now and ask Carly to meet you there."

I quickly called Carly back and told her I was on my way to the park. When I arrived at the park, the atmosphere was quiet and surreal. It was after dark as I pulled into the same parking space Mark, Jr., had used just days before. It was about 10 p.m., and we were the only two people there.

Carly and I walked to the pavilion and sat at the same table where Marky had sat. We hugged, laughed, cried, and encouraged each other. I will never forget the strength and maturity she displayed beyond her sixteen years. I told her how much I loved her and how proud she made me at the memorial service.

As Carly and I sat there at "Marky's table," we talked about him as if he were there with us. I thanked God, quietly to myself, for sending me back there to be with Carly. I am truly blessed to be her father.

It had been an extremely difficult and draining day, but God was still at work. After all, His plan is always infinitely greater than we ever expect. When we simply trust Him and obey His call, when we acknowledge that small voice inside and act on that gentle prompting, we receive much more from God than we could ever have imagined beforehand. I had been asking for more of God's presence during these tough days, and He was delivering, to be sure.

It was now nearly midnight. As Carly and I looked up, we saw six young people walking along the darkened pathways that lead to the pavilion. They arrived simultaneously, in pairs of two, from three different directions. They had heard the news about Marky and were coming to see where he took his last breath. I knew then why God had Carly and me there.

Carly and I asked them to sit at the picnic table. I shared Marky's testimony and the "Celebration of Life" message with them. I asked them if they knew the Lord and each said no. When I asked them if they wanted to accept Jesus as their Lord and Savior, they all replied, "Yes." I looked at Carly and saw tears rolling down her cheeks as she smiled. I asked her to begin the prayer.

God was definitely at work, and all the heavens—Mark, Jr., included—were rejoicing yet again. Carly and I were sitting at the same, exact table where her brother, my son, had just passed away some ninety-four hours earlier, and we were praying as six more souls were saved. These young people had crossed over from death to life in this very place Satan had meant for evil.

MORE LIGHT

After Marky died, many of his friends admitted to me their drug use and the guilt that was accompanying it. One by one, several came to me with stories of their recreational use of a drug called OxyContin.

Edgewood Park and pavilion, Barberton, Ohio (top photo taken in July 2005 at the picnic table where Mark Jr. passed away)

This prescription medication is a seriously addictive painkiller—ten to twenty times stronger and more addictive than other painkillers—known on the streets as "liquid morphine." Marky's stepfather was prescribed it, as was the mother of his friend Nick. Many government entities proved that the manufacturer Purdue Pharma was aware of its illegal usage and the countless thousands of OxyContin addictions and deaths caused by those addictions. The government's lawsuit was quietly settled, yet it allowed Purdue Pharma to continue offering this killer drug to the public. CNNMoney.com reported:

> **Purdue in $634 million settlement over OxyContin**
> **Purdue Pharma to pay $634 million to settle 4-year investigation over OxyContin painkiller marketing.**
>
> July 20 2007: 6:22 PM EDT
>
> NEW YORK (CNNMoney.com)—Purdue Pharma agreed to pay out $634 million to defendants in its OxyContin settlement with federal authorities based in West Virginia. Purdue acknowledged that staffers had violated prescription requirements for its OxyContin painkiller. The company also acknowledged that its "fraudulent conduct caused a greater amount of OxyContin to be available for illegal use than otherwise would has been available."
>
> The drugmaker also said that three "top executives" would be charged with felonies. The company said that it will also be charged with a felony.
>
> The $634 million represents 90 percent of the profits for OxyContin sales during the time of the offense.

I heard statements like "We knew Marky was hooked on Oxys, but he was trying to get off them on his own. He even got a book and tried to quit" and "The drugs helped his anger and temperament issues at first, but he needed stronger and stronger doses for the same effect as time went on."

Marky's involvement with Oxy had started as weekend recreational use. Staying clean during the week permitted him to play high-school baseball at the varsity level throughout the week during that spring and summer, right up until June. He performed well on the field, and this was part of my false sense that everything was okay when I occasionally questioned him about drugs or alcohol.

He batted over .300 (which is a great batting average for those who don't know baseball), and as far as I could tell everything was good. I had no idea that he would be home with the Lord within six weeks.

A WINDOW TO THE SOUL

Months after Marky had passed away, I noticed his eyes looked different in photographs taken just before he went home to the Lord. When he was sixteen years old, his eyes were bright and full of life. By the time he was taken home to heaven, his eyes reflected a hurting and wounded soul. I mistakenly missed that sign. We all did.[30]

Just prior to Marky's passing, he also had been sleeping a lot more often in the afternoons as the painkiller took over his life. Again, we missed this sign as well. We mistakenly thought this was typical summertime behavior for teenagers: late nights hanging out with friends and that sleeping in. That was not the case.

But, as I have mentioned already and as I firmly believe, God makes no mistakes, and Marky now lives life fully without pain or heartache.

MAKE THE CALL!

My relationship with Marky and his friends was always good and open. I was like a father to many of them through the years. They all felt guilty about doing nothing when they knew that Marky had been in trouble. Why hadn't someone called me? Why hadn't one of them told me what was going on? Was the issue not wanting to betray their friend? I explained to them that true friends would not keep the drug abuse and addiction a secret; instead, I taught them, true friends would make sure someone in Marky's situation got help. I did my best to reassure these young people that Marky's death wasn't their fault, but in hopes of preventing further tragedies, I explained that they should have made that call to me, even anonymously.

I explained to Marky's friends that the call could have been as simple as "Mr. Canfora, you don't know me, but your son's in trouble" or "You don't know me, but Marky's hooked on drugs." These young people did listen, and I got that kind of call many times over. In fact, sixteen suicides were prevented that very same year. Make the call as those sixteen lifesavers did.

MARK'S FRIEND

Nick was one of Marky's best friends and one of the many who had accepted Jesus at the funeral services. Yet Nick could not shake the guilt he was feeling, and throughout the funeral services he was visibly upset. He had been the primary supplier, thanks to his mother's prescription meds, and he was involved in the drug use with Marky.

I found this out within a day of Marky's death from another of his friends. My first reaction was anger and rage. I wanted to hurt someone—and hurt him badly.

I called Nick on the phone and asked him to meet me at the park soon after the funeral services. I didn't know what I would do or say, so I prayed for the Lord's guidance. As we walked through the park, Nick was visibly upset, extremely nervous, and very afraid—afraid that his mother would be in trouble, afraid that he was already in trouble.

I took a deep breath. I knew Marky had been his own man who had made his own decisions. He never did anything he didn't want to do. He was a leader, not a follower. I also learned that key to Marky's initial usage was his easy access to his stepfather's pain medications, and he ventured out from there. Nick and friends confirmed that. Still, my pain and anger ran deep. I sat Nick down on the park bench.

I thought, *What would Jesus have me do here? What would Marky have me do here?* I had been an eighteen-year-old once. Even more important, I was—and I am—a forgiven sinner. So…

I forgave Nick.

I cried with Nick, and I hugged him. I also let him know that salvation is real and that he could not deceive God with a false acceptance of Christ. Jesus is real, and so is salvation in Him. God—and only God—knew Nick's heart and whether his commitment to Christ at the funeral services was heartfelt and genuine. Nick and I prayed together and repeated the prayer Carly had led the young people in.

I was at peace. I knew I had done the Lord's will—and Marky would have been pleased. Later that day, I walked through the park with Marky's baseball bat in hand. I had a weapon of warfare, and I don't mean Marky's bat. I had the Word of God and forgiveness in my heart.

Edgewood Park—a place of hope, healing and forgiveness

Dominic (age 5) with Marky's baseball bat poolside July 2005

"THE HEART OF A CHAMPION"

Over the course of the week following the funeral services, I spent all my time at home, and I spent most of that time at the pool. I praised, mourned, played with the children, and wrote down many more instructions from the Lord. After that week, I began fasting for a breakthrough: I was seeking further direction from God. More accurately, I continued my non-eating (I had had no appetite since Marky's passing) rather than actually starting a fast.

During the fast I would wake up regularly between 3:00 and 3:30 a.m., and God would minister to my grieving heart and my contrite spirit. One morning after I had enjoyed hours of praise and worship and just as the sun arose, God told me I was to share the "Celebration of Life" message with others. I then prayed these words: "I want more of You, Lord. I will do as You ask me to do, say what You want me to say, and go where You want me to go."

He showed me how I had already been planting seeds, one at a time and even a few hundred at a time, when I was at the park, at the church services for Marky, and in the graveyard. But God wanted me to see how I could spread that same seed in larger amounts, so He gave me this vision: I saw a large grain sack with millions of tiny seeds in it. Two hands were repeatedly reaching in and grabbing huge quantities of seed, then throwing that seed by the thousands into the field. I asked God about the meaning of this vision, and He replied in one word: *media*. I wrote *MEDIA* in my journal, and then I dated and time-stamped the entry, as I did with every vision, word, sign, revelation, and directive the Lord gave me. It was 7:53 a.m., and at 9:20 a.m. that same morning, my phone rang as I sat in the poolside cabana.

"Hey, Mark, this is Joey." Joey was an old friend from my past life before I came to Christ. When we'd gotten together, we spent time golfing, which then included alcohol or partying. He continued, "I heard about Mark, Jr., and I am so sorry. I also heard about all the people who were saved at the funeral." This was strange talk coming from him! He knew I was saved, but I didn't realize that now he was too. He briefly described his new life in Christ, said he was hosting a radio show in Canton, Ohio, called *Heart of a Champion*, and explained that he wanted me on his program right away.

I thought: *Wow, Lord, You are amazing! Media! The radio and Joey as a way to share the good news of Christ!* I knew this could only be God revealing Himself to me once again!

The radio interview aired early that Saturday morning, and by God's grace it went well. I thanked Joey, who was extremely excited about the way God was moving in my life and using me during this indescribably difficult time. He encouraged me greatly, and he said the inner strength the Lord was providing me encouraged him. I knew God was using Joey to help me act according to some of the instructions I'd written in my journal. Broken before God, I was utterly open before God, and I was receiving from Him grace abundant, grace overflowing.

"A CELEBRATION OF LIFE AND A MESSAGE OF HOPE"

God always has something greater—infinitely greater—than we ever could imagine when we step out in faith. There is no greater example than our salvation. All I knew was that, before, I was sick and tired of being sick and tired of my life—of my old life without peace, without hope, and without God. How much greater has my new life in Christ been than I had expected? It has definitely been *infinitely* greater than I could have ever imagined.

During the summer of Marky's passing and into the fall, we held picnics in the park. Hundreds of people attended, and hundreds committed their life to Christ. And that's when God put it on my heart to have an annual "Celebration of Life" festival at Edgewood Park every July. By God's grace, this park had become a sanctuary, a sacred place, for people—including me—to gather. Edgewood Park had become a church without walls. Even at that point, so soon after Marky's passing, I no longer viewed the park or the pavilion itself as that awful place where my son died, but as the place where he truly began to live. This park was already and continues to be for me the place where Marky lived life as a child, breathed his last earthly breath, and began his eternal life as he instantly left his earthly vessel and was in Jesus' loving arms. So we celebrate life on earth, life in Christ, and our eternal life. Truly, we celebrate life!

We have had a festival each year since 2005—all of them free in Jesus' name. We have basketball tournaments, a home-run derby, fun, food, games, and live music. Thousands have attended, and hundreds have accepted Christ at each annual "Celebration of Life and Message of Hope in Jesus Christ" event. That same park and pavilion where Marky breathed his last earthly breath continues to provide shelter from life's storms and a place for prayer, and many souls are saved at every festival.

God is so great—all the time! I am totally at peace when I am in that very special place.

In April 2009, we had our first annual "Celebration of Life and Family Festival" in Panama City Beach, Florida. Thousands of people attended. Many accepted Christ as Lord and Savior, while many more rededicated their lives to Christ.

THREE CROSSES

In the early days after Marky's passing, one of the things the Lord kept reminding me of was that horrible fifteen-foot metal bar I had cut down from the pavilion. It was still lying on the ground at the park. When I asked the Lord what I should do, He showed me how that bar could be turned into something good. What Satan had intended for harm and evil could be used for some kind of good, to give God glory, because—I was choosing to believe—all things work together for good, for those who love the Lord.

A sense of urgency came over me, and I quickly called my best friend, Bryan, and asked him to drive his van to the park and bring that bar to me. I prayed hard, hoping that it was still lying where I had left it several days before.

It was, so Bryan picked it up that day. I stored it in my barn for several months, waiting on God for further direction....

A friend of mine owns Barberton Steel and Iron, so I had the bar cast into four thirty-pound solid steel crosses and then painted a beautiful gold. We bolted three gold steel crosses onto the center of the larger wooden crosses. Another friend offered his land for the crosses to be erected on. Today they stand strong and mighty along Interstate 76 in Norton, Ohio, where people in over one hundred thousand vehicles a day can easily see them shining brightly, especially as the sun sets on them. Standing tall, they boldly glorify God!

I wrote this on Marky's on-line obituary site at legacy.com on November 2, 2006 the day they were erected:

> Three crosses now stand tall on Interstate 76 and Barber Rd. that symbolize the love Jesus has for us by His death on the cross for all sinners. We have hope that in Christ we are all forgiven, washed clean by the blood of Jesus, and have an eternity in heaven that awaits us.... The crosses are a testimony to God and His love.

What Satan meant for harm . . . now proclaim God's glory

The iron bars that were cast into crosses at the Barberton foundry

And people are noticing. Case in point... On June 4, 2009, I got a voice-mail message from my cousin, Don, whom I hadn't talked to in over a year. (He is the same cousin who gave me the Sawzall to cut down the bar in the pavilion some forty-seven months earlier.)

"Hey, I just had to tell you I was headed east on I-76, and it's a beauti-ful sunny day. It's about 75 degrees, and I looked over at the three crosses and thought of you and Marky. Yeah, oh man, the sun was shining right on them, and they were gleaming! I just had to call you and see how you are doing. We love ya. I'm on my way with my kids to the Kenmore car-nival. We'll see you at the festival at Edgewood when you come home to Ohio in July. Call me."

All things work together for good—to make us more like Christ—for those of us who love God! *All things* even includes that bar Satan tempted my son to use to squeeze the last breath from his body.[31]

The fourth cross is placed on the stage at our festival events. To God be the glory!

14

Following God's Call

God woke me up again at 3:30 in the morning, and I flipped the television on to TBN. Dynamic evangelist Paula White was enthusiastically speaking into the camera about the upcoming T. D. Jakes' 2005 MegaFest. Over one hundred thousand people were expected to be in attendance....

I was still fasting and continuing to hear from the Lord morning, noon, and in the middle of the night. He was giving every event, conversation, and detail in my life meaning and impact. No demons or principalities could begin to contend with this work of God.

I had experienced many things during the previous two weeks. My own son's death had brought me into a realm where nothing distracted me from God, and I gained an amazingly profound understanding of Jesus' shed-blood sacrifice for me, for my son, for all of mankind. I was deeply "in the valley of the shadow of death." As I fasted and grieved, I was praying, praising, and seeking God's will and direction. I "fear[ed] no evil." God's rod and His staff were comforting me, and He was mightily revealing Himself to me. I had a broken heart and a contrite spirit; I had a broken spirit and a contrite heart. I was a wounded, hurting child of God greatly in need of my Father, and He answered mightily once again.

"Go to Atlanta and receive what I have for you!" I heard in my spirit. The words Paula White spoke on that early-morning television show resonated deep in my heart and soul. The heart of her message was about healing, a ministry calling, spiritual warfare, and getting direction from

God. These were words for me, and I knew I needed to go to Atlanta—and God confirmed it in just a few short hours....

Joey called me at 8:15. As usual, I was at my poolside sanctuary, in the cabana house, when Joey excitedly reported, "Mark, I was watching TBN last night and Paula White was on. . . ."

I interrupted him, saying, "So did I, and I'm going to MegaFest."

He heartily laughed out loud and said, "Let's go! The Lord said for us to go. I'll be there in an hour."

When Joey picked me up for the twelve-hour drive, he was driving an early-nineties Corvette. As I sat in the front seat for the drive to Atlanta, I reflected on the vision of scattering seed and the "Media!" message when I noticed the Corvette emblem right in front of me on the dashboard. I smiled and thought to myself, *Thank You, Lord. You are so, so awesome.* The Corvette was Marky's favorite car!

We arrived at MegaFest that night. Joey had called ahead and arranged media passes for us, and within minutes of our arrival, we were standing among MegaFest leaders and ministries like T.D. Jakes of The Potter's House, Paula White, her son Brandon and family, Bishop Eddie Long, and Kirk Franklin, and Trinity Broadcasting Network, that reaches every country in the world, was there as well. God was definitely moving. Less than twenty-four hours earlier I had been watching Paula White on TBN, and now Joey and I were standing in the same room with her.

Within a few short minutes, one by one, they noticed my "Mark, Jr., R.I.P. 1986-2005" T-shirt with his photo on it, and they asked about him. I told them that just a few weeks ago he had gone home to the Lord, and a ministry had been birthed: "A Celebration of Life and Message of Hope." I talked about the souls saved at the funeral services, and I shared Marky's testimony.

On two different occasions, two eighteen-year-olds—Brandon Crouch, the grandson of TBN founder Paul and Jan Crouch, and Brandon White, son of Paula White—laid hands on my shoulders and my heart. They boldly prayed, speaking life into our ministry and healing for my grieving heart.

Just a few nights earlier, God had prophesied through one of our church leaders that I would adopt one thousand sons in the spirit while still on this earth. Both of these eighteen-year-olds—the same age as Mark, Jr.—said the same thing, reassuring me both that Marky is at peace in heaven and that our ministry would reach millions of people all over the globe. I had in my hand five hundred fliers with information about our ministry. I was seeing God work mightily—and once again, He was only just beginning.

THEY KNEW MY PAIN

Besides introducing me to the world's the largest media group, ministries, and prayer chains at MegaFest, God had something especially for me. He had one-hundred-thousand-plus poor, hurting, and suffering mothers, grandmothers, sisters, brothers, parents, and children who knew the kind of pain I was in. They knew pain from their own unique experiences, and they showed me compassion both one-on-one and in large groups. They knew the pain of death, poverty, imprisonment, and loss. No one knew better than they. Their heritage of dealing with abuse, prejudice, and injustice had taught them that God was, is, and will always be their Refuge and Deliverer. Asked who Jesus is to them, the vast majority of older black women will say, "He is everything to me. He is my Lord and my Savior!" Men, women, and children there at MegaFest knew and felt my pain as we laughed, cried, and encouraged one another in the Lord.

I attended as many events as I possibly could during those two days. Many strong prayer warriors and women of amazing spiritual resolve spoke tremendous and powerful prayers over me and our newly birthed ministry, a ministry birthed in tears.[32] I gave each a flier and asked them to put Celebration of Life on their prayer chains and in their prayers. I estimate that prayer for our ministry—through the media outlets and the individual churches represented there—went out to forty states and over one hundred countries.

As Joey and I walked through the Georgia Dome after midnight on our last night, I had only a few ministry fliers left, and we were exhausted. I was still fasting and praying. I was definitely running only on God's strength, and He was still moving mightily.

Four young men and a mother approached us in the lobby, and we greeted each other. When they saw my shirt, I wearily told my story once again. They were a Christian Gospel hip-hop and rap group called The Perfect Combo. We exchanged prayers, words, and hugs. I gave them a flier about our ministry, and they signed a CD, dedicating it to Marky and the ministry. (The CD was awesome. Jonathan Brewster, aka

SM Souljah— Single-Minded Soldier for Christ—from Killeen, Texas, truly has an amazing ministry. God has gifted him to combat secular rap music and its garbage lyrics. His music has a great beat and, more importantly, words that glorify God.) Joey and I left for our hotel and then went back to Ohio. God would reveal His purpose for that midnight meeting... two years later.

09/08/86 MARKY *AND* JONATHAN

One year later, in July 2006, we had our first Celebration of Life Festival at Edgewood Park, and over seven hundred and fifty people attended and over one hundred were saved. The next year, in the spring of 2007, I was praying in my office for a feature band for the second annual festival.

Just then my son Dominic—seven at the time—came walking down the hallway singing, "I'm dropping rhymes for the One that gave His life; I'm dropping rhymes for the One that gave His life, yo." I thought to myself, *OK, Lord, I get it.* Dom's song was such a sweet rendition of a cut from The Perfect Combo CD. I excitedly called the number on the CD cover. Jonathan "SM Souljah" answered.

"Hey, this is Mark Canfora, and I met you at MegaFest 2005 in the Georgia Dome. You gave me a CD."

He hesitated as he thought back. "Oh yeah, I remember you. You had a son who passed away. I still have your flier, and I've prayed for you and your ministry."

We talked for a few moments, and I told him about the festivals and what God had been doing in the ministry since MegaFest. I asked him to join us in Ohio on July 7, 2007.

He said he would go to our Web site and pray about it. SM Souljah called back the next day and said, "Mr. Canfora, you won't believe this. I looked at the flier, and Mark, Jr., and I were born on the same day, September 8. Listen to this: not only the same day, but the same year. Yeah, man, 1986. I will be honored to do your festival! This is all God!"

The fulfillment of prophecy continues: a thousand sons adopted in the Spirit. Jonathan had been knit in his mother's womb at the same exact time Marky was. God knew the day, the hour, when Marky and Jonathan would be born and the day, the hour, when Souljah and I would meet in the Georgia Dome. By God's grace, He had preordained our meeting from the beginning of time.[33]

Mark Canfora Sr. at Megafest 2005

Joey and I in the Georgia Dome Megafest 2005

Jonathon Brewster (Sm Souljah), Mark Canfora Sr., and Angelo (L.I.L.L.O.) Celebration of Life and Family Festival, Panama City Beach, Florida, 2009

SM Souljah and The Perfect Combo played at our second annual Celebration of Life Festival and again, on April 11, 2009, in Panama City Beach, Florida at The Celebration of Life and Family Festival.

Before his first appearance with us, SM Souljah wrote the song "I've Got Hope" for the ministry, and presented it to me at the 2007 festival in the park. (Photos and songs are on our Web site at www.IveGotHope.com; songs of hope are also listed in Appendix D.) Jonathan will always have a special place in my heart as my adopted son in the Spirit—one of the thousand sons God has given me just as He promised.

God is so, so awesome, and He is in control.

SIXTEEN SUICIDES PREVENTED

After MegaFest 2005 and throughout the next year, I continued to seek God with all my heart, mind, soul, and spirit. We held regular youth gatherings at our church, The Father's House. Several hundred more youth were saved, and lives were dramatically changed for Christ. The spiritual warfare continued in our community, and, sadly, many of the youth who accepted Jesus as their Savior failed to make Him Lord of their lives…

I had always been a father that Marky's friends knew and enjoyed being around. At the park, I regularly played baseball, basketball, and tennis with them, and I attended their games. For years before Marky's passing, I had talked openly with them at the park about school, about girls, about the Lord, about anything they wanted to talk about.

That role—of being someone kids can talk to—continued. At the festivals and whenever I spoke, I regularly encouraged young people and their parents to "make the call" when someone they knew was in serious trouble—and people did make the calls. On sixteen separate occasions during the first year of the Celebration of Life and Message of Hope Ministry, I received phone calls letting me know that several of Marky's friends were talking about or intending to commit suicide. Our immediate concern was for this circle of Marky's closest friends, and we were ready to respond. Most calls came at night, and on one very frightening occasion, a friend of Marky's had a gun and had placed rope around his neck at a party at 4 a.m. Whenever the phone call came, I immediately intervened and met with the young person. I spoke to him or her about the pain and suffering suicide would cause their friends and loved ones, and I always closed by asking for permission to tell their parents.

The phone call to the parents went something like this: "I'm Mark Canfora, Sr., and I recently spoke with your son/daughter. This is the phone call I wish I would have received before my child Mark, Jr., passed away." I would explain the circumstances and plead with the parents to get help for their child. In each and every case, these young people abandoned the thought of ending their life.

DREAMS, VISIONS, SIGNS, WONDERS, AND ANGELS

After several months, I was so involved in the ministry that my personal life as well as my business began to suffer. Having let my priorities get out of order, I was off God's path for my life. I was trying to do too much—and often in my own power, in my own timing, and according to my own agenda—and God knew it. Yet many times, during the course of that first year—and still to this day—God intervened in my life through dreams, visions, signs, wonders, and angels. Yes, angels. I'll get to that in a minute.

God cannot violate His spiritual laws and the ways He established for mankind since the fall of Adam and Eve. He won't send Mark, Jr., to me, today, in the flesh, and violate either His plan for us or the laws of His created universe. But in line with His promises, God will give us signs, wonders, dreams, and visions to guide and encourage us. We will receive God-inspired messages through various individuals, experiences, and nature itself. I truly believe that dreams and visions are two of God's many spiritual languages, two of the many ways we can hear from God. I also believe that He speaks to us through the people He puts in our path.

To this day, for instance, I still feed the homeless and pray with them on the streets. People regularly come to realize their sin and their need for Jesus in gas stations, real estate offices, street corners, batting cages, on the beach, at festivals, and annually in Edgewood Park. And on many occasions, the lost, hurting, and homeless man, woman, or child will give me a word from God that could only be from Him.

God always shows up right on time, exactly when I need it the most. How do I know when a conversation is ordained by God and the words I hear are from Him? I know by the person's voice and eyes; I know as the person's countenance changes during the message relayed to me. I have watched the uneducated and normally garbled speech of complete strangers become articulate and clearly spoken. Words flow from their mouths straight from heaven. Their once-distant eyes become clear. We talk, we laugh, we cry, we hug, we pray, and I walk away thanking and praising God for knowing my name, for loving me, and revealing Himself to me at that moment in time. He moves in my life. He loves me.

MINISTERING ANGELS

As I mentioned, I have on several occasions been ministered to by what I believe to be angels.

I attended the Cherry Street Revival festival for the poor in downtown Canton, Ohio. Joey and his Heart of a Champion Ministry were inspired to sponsor this event after attending one of our celebration festivals. On the last night I was tired, and I really didn't want to go. I had given a message the day before, and my wife, Dena, had led worship. I selfishly felt I had done my part.

But I started the forty-minute drive from home because the Lord spoke to me to go down to Canton one more time. I changed my mind en route and headed back home. I *really* didn't want to go, but I finally decided to obey God's prompting. I made another U-turn in the middle of the highway and headed back toward the revival.

I got there for the last hour and sat in the back of the tent. I was upset and feeling sorry for myself. I was feeling bitter and tired, and I was missing my son. I didn't even stand for the final praise and worship songs, led by my Pastor Mike and our worship team. Most of the time I was there, I was complaining to God.

When the program was over—and it was almost midnight—I started to help break everything down. I was still asking God why He had sent me there as I watched a seemingly homeless man come near. Everyone was done and anxious to leave. I don't believe anyone noticed the man except me. His speech was severely slurred, yet he seemed agitated. The agitation was understandable. We were in a very rough area of downtown Canton; drug dealers and prostitutes were everywhere on the streets.

I thought, *All right, God. Is this why You sent me here? Okay, I'm ready.* I begrudgingly walked up to the man. "May I pray with you?" When he nodded his head yes, I placed my hand on his shoulder and prayed a short prayer—and I thought we were through.

Then this man asked if he could pray. When I agreed, he dropped to the ground, kneeling with perfect posture, hands pressed together, and eyes looking toward heaven. In a clear voice, he said simply and very articulately, "I pray that every person in the world accepts You, Jesus, as their Lord and Savior. Amen."

When he arose, I asked him if he had a message for me, and he said he did. When we were interrupted by everyone leaving, I offered him a ride home. I wanted to hear this message from the Lord. I knew that God had sent me there for this message, and I wanted to hear it. Yet the people who heard my offer were concerned for my safety, but they knew I had eight-plus years of street-ministry experience and felt streetwise enough to take care of myself.

During the ride, this man fell back into his garbled speech patterns and agitated behaviors, and Satan sowed seeds of fear in my mind. I pressed the man for the message from the Lord. "Wait," he said. "Wait and I'll tell you." I decided to stop the car, and I looked right into the man's glossed-over eyes and said firmly, "God knows the day and hour I am going home to the Lord, not you or Satan. There is nothing you can do to harm me that God Himself has not allowed."

He immediately became quiet, and I drove him into a projects area in South Canton. The neighborhood was dark and dirty. As he started to get out of the car, he turned and looked right into my eyes. At that moment he was a man of complete composure, his eyes were as clear as crystal, and he spoke one word: "Obey!"

I was breathless and in awe of the Lord as I drove home. I know God sends angels,[34] and I know that He speaks through all types of people. God is no respecter of persons, and He is always on time.

"IT'S ALL THE DANCING, DAD!"

In addition to using signs, wonders, and angels, God also speaks in dreams just as He promised.[35] The first truly notable dream of Marky I had came on April 12, 2006, nine months to the day after his entry into heaven.

In the dream, I was in heaven, and Marky came walking toward me. I had dreamed about Marky prior to this, but not one of those dreams was as real or vivid as this one. The colors and brightness were intense, and I had never seen anything like this place on earth or in my dreams.

As Marky approached me, I began to cry and stretched out my arms toward him. God always allowed me to see him in his earthly body. However, in this dream, his body was different. His complexion and eyes were unbelievably bright and clear. His smile was radiant, and he was at peace.

As we hugged each other tightly and I kissed his cheek, his body began to disappear. Yet I stood with my arms stretched upward as if I were holding onto Marky's spirit as it grew larger and larger until the area we were in could not contain it.

Still reaching upward and still trying to hold on to Marky, I looked over to my right and saw a large gathering of people looking at me, and I began to cry. "It's my son. I miss my son." After I said those words, they understood why I was there and continued on their way.

I looked back up, my arms still reaching high, and said, "Marky, you're so big. How did you get so big? You always said you'd be bigger than me." Ever since he could walk and talk, Marky always said he would grow up to be taller than me—and at least six feet tall. We joked regularly about that, and as he grew to be 5'7", he was—much to his disappointment—still an inch shorter than me.

Marky answered, "It's all the dancing, Dad. It's all the dancing!"

It was just after midnight, and as I awoke, I began to sob loudly. These were tears of joy. My wife could hear me from downstairs and several hundred feet away at the other end of the house. She came running, and I explained what had happened. Dena was relieved that everything was all right, but my account of the dream startled her.

For me, though, the dream's message produced tears of joy and cries of hope. These were tears of father who has just received a message from God that his child is experiencing no more pain, suffering, anxiety, or heartache—and would never experience those things again. I had been blessed with a God-given dream in which I was able to hold, speak, kiss, and talk to my child in heaven. It was a gift of pure joy, love, hope, and peace. I knew the message of the dream was absolutely true, and I knew that God had given me this special dream, this special encounter with my son. I later realized that this moment marked a birthing for me at, appropriately enough, this nine-month point in my life of recovery—a birth to a whole new level of hope and direction; a whole new place on the healing journey.

I knew this dream was from God. Why was I sure? Because as far as any of us know Marky never danced a step in his life. He was a phenomenal athlete, but he was definitely not a dancer.

I also know this dream was God-given, because if I were screenwriting the dream, Marky would have said, "It's all the weight lifting and working out, Dad. It's the baseball and the basketball that made me so big and strong."

But this was of the Lord. "It's all that the dancing, Dad. It's all the dancing!"

My son, all children, and any who have passed away having named Jesus as their Lord and Savior dance in heaven with the angels. And they grow stronger and they live life abundantly.

THE RIVER OF LIFE

In another dream, I was sitting on the bank of what I believe was heaven's River of Life. I was with my mother-in-law Linda while Marky was swimming. It was the most beautiful, crystal-clear, shimmering water I had ever seen. In another few moments, Marky walked up the riverbank with a towel wrapped around his waist. His complexion was white and pure; his eyes glistened with peace. I anxiously awaited his arrival, and he climbed onto my lap and hugged and kissed me. "I love you, Dad." Like in the other dream, as I was holding him, his body disappeared and I was left holding the air—his spirit. I don't pretend to have all the answers about heaven, but based on what I have seen, it will be glorious.

I awoke once again, quietly crying to myself as tears of joy ran onto my pillow. I whispered, "Thank You, Lord."

A FORTY-DAY FAST

After the dream in April 2006, the "dancing" dream, I prayed heartily and asked the Lord for direction. I had a new peace, and I wanted to know "Where do I go from here? Where does my family go from here?"

I had fasted before for stretches of fourteen and even twenty-one days before. After all, the Bible says clearly some demonic attacks, some moving of mountains, and some spiritual warfare require fasting and prayer.[36] I sensed it was time to fast again, so I did.

During the fast, and at a point when I was tremendously weak and full of doubts, I had another dream—a dream unlike anything I had ever experienced in my life, awake or asleep. In the dream I was sitting in the back corner of a church. Walking down the center aisle, from the front of the church to the back, was Jesus Himself, and He was wearing the most beautiful white robe, flowing from His shoulders to the floor. As He walked toward the rear of the church, He was praying, and I knew

He was coming to me. The closer He got, the more still I became. As I sat there motionless, Jesus walked toward me, and I looked for His face and saw that the hood of His robe now covered His head.

As He stood before me, I could and did look directly into His face. When He lifted His head, my eyes looked into His, and I saw eternity. I could see the most magnificent, beautiful light, bright and clear. His eyes were crystal clear, and He had the most amazing complexion. I wasn't afraid, but I was speechless and motionless. As He approached me, He raised His hands, placed them on my cheeks, and said, "Obey." I sat there awestruck, and as I was awaking from the dream, I heard Him say, "Psalm 119."

It was about 7 a.m., and I reached for my Bible on CD next to my bed as I woke Dena. "I had the most awesome dream. Jesus held my face in His hands and said, 'Obey . . . Psalm 119.'" I placed the CD with Psalm 119 in my player; and "Obey my precepts, obey my commands, obey my laws, obey my decrees" sounded over and over one hundred and seventy times.

Psalm 119 was not a chapter I had known well or ever studied much. It is the longest psalm in the book, and it takes seventeen minutes to play on a CD. But since this was God speaking, I vowed to obey, to answer this call on my life. Here are the first few verses I heard that early morning as Dena and I entered a whole new place in the Lord, in our marriage, in our family:

> *Blessed are they whose ways are blameless,*
>   *who walk according to the law of the* LORD.
>
> Blessed are they who *keep his statutes*
>   and seek him with all their heart.
>
> They do nothing wrong;
>   they *walk in his ways.*
>
> You have laid down precepts
>   that are to be *fully obeyed.*
>
> Oh, that my ways were steadfast
>   in *obeying your decrees!*
>   PSALM 119:1-5 NIV, EMPHASIS MINE

I knew I could never obey God's commands, statutes, decrees, and laws in my own strength. But we can obey when, by abiding in Him and trusting in Him, we draw on His strength. Then He can and will do His work in us and through our lives.[37]

A NEW PLACE

Soon after that dream, on the thirty-third day of my fast, I was introduced to a major Ohio real estate developer who needed help on his construction project in Panama City Beach, Florida. Within days, my wife and I were in Florida. I soon signed a contract and planned to move my family there in July 2006 after our first festival in the park.

How did my wife and I know this opportunity was what the Lord wanted us to do? Because it was the last thing we ever would have done on our own! Because our entire family, church, ministry, business—everything was in Ohio! Moving out of state and starting anew was totally God's plan, not at all ours. We struggled for a few days with the decision, and then we both came—individually and together—to a point of peace. We were on a journey—a healing and strengthening journey—that God knew we needed.

During the forty-eight months since Mark, Jr., went home to be with the Lord, I have drifted briefly out of God's will for my life. At times I haven't always obeyed His precepts and laws, and many times I have doubted His plans for my life and felt sorry for myself. I can't stay in that place very long because I become physically and spiritually ill.

God always gently gets me back on His path, His narrow path. I now know from experience what Jesus meant by "narrow is the path to life and wide is the road to destruction."[38] Thankfully, God nudges me back on His path through His Holy Spirit. I do not need to be prompted by the feelings, emotions, or pull of this world. I can—and I have to—walk in the Spirit, not in the flesh. We are in this world, but not of it. The worries of this world no longer choke the Word of God out of my life. I have been to the valley of the shadow of death and seen mountains moved. I will always have a foot in that valley until I am home with my Lord and Savior—and with Marky, a *treasure that awaits me in heaven.*

I have experienced life. I have been touched by death. I have seen prayers answered by God. I have been blessed with dreams, signs, and wonders. God has given me five wonderful children, a beautiful wife, and loving family and friends. But I would not trade anything for my salvation and my faith in the Lord Jesus Christ. He is my Rock. He is my Refuge. He is my Strength. Jesus is everything to me.

He can be your Rock, your Refuge, your Strength, your Everything if you simply accept His free gift of salvation and allow Him to be the Lord and Savior of your life.

TEARS AND BLESSINGS

Many times as I've been writing this book, I have stopped to wipe the tears from my eyes. Reliving the experience of deep pain, heartache, and suffering is not easy. The memories from that early morning on July 12, 2005, are still so fresh.

It is now the fall of 2009. This four-year journey has been filled with evidence of God working in my life and answering my prayers. It is only by God's will, strength, and guidance that I am able to type these words. So, acting on my faith in God and my love for Him, I hope and pray that this book will help and encourage others who suffer the shocking loss and excruciatingly painful tragedy of the death of a loved one, especially the death of a child.

I close this chapter with an important truth... My now nine-year-old son, Dominic, and I regularly walk the beaches of Panama City Beach singing his favorite song. In fact, as I was writing this book, he scrawled out in red crayon the words from that song, and they sit before me, on my office wall, as I write:

Lord, prepare me
To be a sanctuary
Pure and holy
Tried and true
With thanksgiving
I'll be a living
Sanctuary for you.

God is so, so good... all the time. I count my blessings daily.

Dominic and I on the beach in 2007

The Canfora Family Christmas 2004: Carly, Marky, Mark Sr., Dena, Juliana, Dominic, and Brooke

Lord prepare
me to be A

Sanctuary pure
and holy tried
and true. With
Thanksgiving I'll
be a living
Sanctuary for you

Dominic 12-15-08

PART TWO

15

The Pathway to the Park

So what happened to Marky that caused him to turn to drugs for his pain and ultimately die, all alone in a park, in the middle of the night? In these final chapters, I want to describe for you the pathway to the park that we, as a family, had traveled so that you might recognize any telltale signs and avoid the destination we arrived at.

I also want to address a few other questions in hopes that you and your family might enjoy a closer, richer walk with the God who loves you enough to let His only Son die for you. Those questions are *How did I get to the point I expect to receive an answer when I talk to God?; What brought me to this place in life where I look to God and find strength in Him?;* and *How have I learned to recognize God's voice when He is speaking to me in a vision or dream or through someone?* Let's get started.

GOD HAS A PLAN

First of all, an important basic: I believe God has a plan for my life that is unlike His plan for any other life ever lived on this earth. I also believe that God has a unique call on your life and that no two lives are exactly the same. Every person's life, every person's calling, is totally unique.[39] As I look back over my life, I clearly see how true these statements are—and they are true to the degree to which we seek and ask God to be real in our lives, to the degree that we really want to know and trust Him.

As I look back on my life, I clearly see how God is always present and always waiting on us to seek Him. I appreciate more today than ever His profound desire to have a relationship with us. He gives us the free will to choose to walk through life with Him and to obey His commands. Our heavenly Father will never force us to have that relationship with Him, but as is any good Father, He is always there for me—and for you.

Despite His faithful ever-presence with us, I found that in the midst of this nightmare—this storm of emotions following Marky's suicide—I had questions that God did not immediately answer. Yet as I took one step of faith at a time, He, according to the pace of His perfect plan for me, revealed many answers to my questions—on one condition: I needed to trust Him and obey Him. I realize now that we will never totally know or understand all the reasons why God permits tragedies to happen. Some things are only to be revealed upon our arrival in heaven and not before. I am at peace with that reality now. After all, God's ways are definitely higher than my ways.[40]

A KEY DISTINCTION: GOD, JESUS, AND RELIGION

Now back to the beginning of my life, the beginning of my journey...

I am the youngest child of four, and I was raised in a middle-class Italian/Slovak family. My father, Albert, worked at Goodyear Aerospace and was a top union leader. A full-blooded Italian, he was raised by immigrant parents who met on the boat coming from Naples, Italy, to the United States in 1920. My mother, Anna, is half Czechoslovakian and half Austrian, and she is a full-time homemaker. She was raised on a farm in New Brighton, Pennsylvania, along with her nine brothers and sisters. Our family lived in Barberton, Ohio, a blue-collar town located in northeast Ohio near Akron and sandwiched between Canton and Cleveland. My family was always active in politics, my dad was a city councilman, and, like 90 percent of our town, we were strong Democrats and union members.

The first major change in my life came on May 4, 1970, when I was twelve years old. I came home from my sixth-grade class at Decker Elementary School in Barberton, Ohio, to find our house filled with people in the living room and spilling out onto the front porch. My seventeen-year-old brother, Sonny, met me on the sidewalk with news that was shocking—especially if you are twelve years old.

As I neared the porch, Sonny shouted excitedly, "Alan was shot at

My oldest brother Alan, waving a black flag at Kent State University on May 4 1970, just moments prior to shootings that killed four students and wounded nine. (Photo courtesy of John Filo)

The Canfora Family: (Back Row): Ian (nephew), Sonny, Chic, Dad and Mom, Mark Sr., Dena, Brooke, Alan; (Front Row): Carly, Natalie (niece), Dominic, Michael (nephew), Juliana (not pictured: Marky in Heaven) Christmas 2009

college today!"

"What?"

"He was shot at Kent State! He was wounded—shot in the right wrist—and Chicky was there. She hid behind some cars, and she almost was shot too. Four kids are dead, and a bunch more wounded. Alan is in the living room."

I walked into the living room that was packed full of people. Alan sat on the couch. His right wrist was bandaged, and I could see the blood stains seeping through. The TV was turned up unusually loud as Alan, his college friends, my sister, Mom, and Dad all watched the news.

Dorothy Fuldheim, the local news anchor and a Midwest icon, was crying. News clips showed the tear gas and the National Guard soldiers who fired the shots. She was saying that this was the most tragic day she could remember: "We, as a government, were killing our own children."

Later, it would be confirmed that four students were dead and nine wounded, all shot by high-powered M-1 rifles. It would take seven years of trials before the families received some resemblance of justice in the matter, before the FBI and other government investigators determined the shootings to be "unjustifiable, inexcusable, and unwarranted." After civil litigation, the government gave the parents of the four slain students $15,000 for each life lost, which they in turn donated to a paraplegic survivor of the shootings.

This tragic event would soon prove my escape, my ticket out of the church and religion as I knew it. The following day the priest from our church was in our living room, and he proceeded to tell us, in his broken Hungarian accent, about his ethnic roots in a communist European country. He adamantly explained to us that my brother, my sister, and the other students had no right to protest against the government or the war in Vietnam. The priest suggested that we support the actions of our country whether we liked them or not. If we didn't like our country, then we should leave it. My mother, who is truly the backbone and strength of our family, politely but firmly escorted the priest off our property, and we never attended that church or any other church again.

My family knew the tragedies of communism from our own European heritage. We also deeply loved America and the freedoms we enjoy, including the First Amendment right to freedom of speech; freedoms my father fought for during World War II, freedoms that cost him his right eye while serving his country; and freedoms my mother stood for as an Army nurse during that same war. As I mentioned previously, my mom was my dad's nurse in 1944 as he recovered from his eye surgery. My dad says, "I lost an eye and gained a wife." They have been happily married for sixty-one years.

After the priest left, I thought to myself, *No more Saturday morning religion classes, and now I can play football on Sunday mornings!* I was much too young to understand much about "religion" or to recognize the priest's misguided attempt to discuss democracy and freedom of speech. Thus began a very emotional roller-coaster ride and my painful twenty-seven-year journey to the realization that manmade religion and mistakes made in the name of that religion do not at all reflect who God is or His purpose for our life.

TRUE CHRISTIANITY IN ACTION

In early 1997, I was doing my monthly "social mission work" in the housing projects, because it made me feel good (but usually just for that one day). I wasn't offering these poor families and children any hope or way out of their miserable circumstances. I only had some things they needed in their lives at that particular moment.

I was diligently trying to earn my way into heaven by working at those projects, and that's when God placed Pastor Mike Guarnieri from Grace Fellowship Church directly in my path. He was there passing out bags of groceries—and hope, I learned later—to the poor. As if I were protecting my people, my territory, I approached him and asked, "Who are you?"

Who is this man? I thought. *Probably a Jehovah's Witness or someone like that having the nerve to come into my area! These are* my *housing projects, and these are* my *poor.*

He said, "Hi, I'm Pastor Mike. Who are you?"

"I'm Mark," I answered sassily. "What is it that you are doing here?"

He answered, "Giving away groceries."

"Where are you from?" I shot back.

"Grace Fellowship, and we've been coming here for the last eight years, clothing and feeding the people who live here."

I was completely taken aback. Here was a senior pastor, with his sleeves rolled up, feeding the poor. I was very impressed.

As I helped him and his volunteers unload the groceries, I told them about my past efforts in the housing projects. The pastor graciously invited me to his church only a few blocks away.

I liked what I saw, and I was impressed by his servant heart. He was a pastor—*and* he fed the poor. That was all I needed! I went home with the cool news for my wife, and it turned out that this was my mother-in-law's pastor and church. I attended several services and, for the first time in my life, heard the Word of God preached by a true man of God who loved the Lord with all his heart. And he definitely walked the walk.

On May 31, 1997, just a couple months after meeting Pastor Mike and attending several of his services, I took a step that would change my life forever. Deep down inside I had been praying for a serious change in my life....

When I couldn't make the usual Saturday delivery of a van full of children's items for the poor, Pastor Mike agreed to pass out the donations for me. We agreed to meet at the church so I could let them use the van. As we talked briefly in the church basement, I quizzed him on some things I didn't understand about God. I thanked him for his time and, as I was leaving, he said something that would forever change my life.

"You know, Mark, you can give thousands of van loads of food, clothes, and toys to the poor, but even that good work will never fill that void that is in your heart. Only Jesus Christ can fill that. God loves you, and He wants a relationship with you through His Son Jesus Christ." Nodding my head up and down, as though I understood, I turned to walk out the door, but I couldn't take another step forward. I turned back to Pastor Mike and said, "I'm ready. I want to accept Jesus as my Savior."

I walked back to the table and sat down. Pastor Mike had mist in his eyes that sparkled, and he smiled as he prayed Romans 10:9-10.

If you confess with your mouth, "Jesus is Lord," and believe in your heart that God raised him from the dead, you will be saved. For it is with your heart that you believe and are justified, and it is with your mouth that you confess and are saved.

As I look back, I realize more and more clearly how God had been preparing me for these valley times—for Marky's passing and these four years since—for several years. This life-changing encounter with Pastor

Mike is just one example.

Second, after naming Jesus my Savior and Lord, I diligently and for the first time ever, read the Bible. In fact, I read through the entire Bible the first year I was a Christian, and I also spent time listening to God's Word. I read and I re-read and I regularly listened to the New Testament on CD—over and over. As I devoured God's Word and fed my spirit, I grew stronger by the day. The words of Scripture gripped me like never before. It was as if I had found the greatest secret for living life, and I went after it with all my heart, mind, soul, and spirit. And everyone around me witnessed a remarkable change in me, change for the good. Because of the work of God's Spirit in my heart, Bible passages were changing my life. Slowly, I was becoming a new creation in Christ.[41]

I was on fire for the Lord. Christ had indeed filled the void in my heart, and now, when I served the poor, I was doing it for Jesus and His glory. I no longer served in the housing projects in order to feel better about myself. I served in order to offer hope in Jesus' almighty Name!

WHAT LOVE IS

I learned about the great sacrifice God had given us in Jesus, His only Son who was crucified for our sins—for mine and for yours. As an act of love for us, the sinless Jesus gave His life as a ransom for us. He laid down His life for the salvation of the world.[42]

After we accept this truth about Christ and invite Him into our lives as Lord and Savior, we must learn to love as He loved.[43] Salvation is the believer's starting point. Then we must, by the power of His Holy Spirit, learn to willingly lay down our life for other people. We need to share the good news of Christ and His love through our actions, not just with our words. We are to be servants and have servant's hearts for others. We are to fight for justice, defend the poor, help the homeless, serve the widows, and come alongside the fatherless and downtrodden. I also learned to fast and I learned to pray. As I attended Pastor Mike's Spirit-filled church that believed in all the gifts of the Spirit, I grew stronger in Christ.

Clearly, for eight years, God had been preparing me for the battle of my life. He rewarded my mustard seed of faith when He met me in those early morning hours after Marky passed away. He answered me when I laid hands across Marky's chest and asked Him to raise my son, to breathe life into him, to let him live.

You may be reading this and thinking that I was—or even still am—delusional; that I am out of my mind for even beginning to believe God can be so real to us. But I am here to testify that I was crushed by Marky's death, I needed help, and God answered my cries. I am a survivor of incredible pain and a living testimony to God's work in my life—and I have even more of His work to tell you about. At this point, I want to make one thing clear: I know that I know.

Unzipping that body bag and asking God to let my son live was the start of my new relationship with God. He continues to draw closer to me as I study His Word, live according to His precepts, and follow His direction for my life. More than anything, that desperate, purposeful act of faith at the morgue—that cry of this heartbroken father, of one of God's children—got that mountain of pain that came with Marky's death moving. By that one simple act of faith—by my asking God to be my strength—this mountain that once towered over my life has been moved, leveled, and destroyed!

Furthermore, I believe that, as an act of love for me, God has revealed to me one reason why He chose to have Marky's days number 6,870. Here is why God chose to let Marky live at his birth, to be a shining light into mine, and to bring God's light into the life of almost everyone he touched and continues to touch: *God's love, truth, and hope have been revealed through this tragedy*. The all-important message has been shared, the message that salvation from the consequences of one's sin is available because of the death and resurrection of Jesus, and literally thousands have accepted that invitation into the Lord's family since that tragic morning.

The battle had intensified several years earlier when, in that southern Ohio hotel room, I had considered suicide myself: at that point Satan had me halfway devoured and literally minutes from an eternity in hell. But by God's grace I had reached out for God, and He had been there for me. God had snatched me from the jaws of the enemy when I cried out to Him.

A BATTLE IN THE HEAVENLY REALM

Back in 1997, when I turned around, walked back into that church basement, and told Pastor Mike that I was ready to accept Jesus Christ as my Lord and Savior, the battle for my family began in the heavenly realm. Truly unbeknownst to me—or my family or even Pastor Mike, despite his extensive knowledge of God's Word—the battle for my life, my wife and marriage, and our children's lives that was about to commence. After all, such life-and-death battles between God's angels and Satan's demons rage continuously in the heavens.

God had a call on my life, and I finally responded: at age thirty-nine, I accepted Jesus as my Lord and Savior. I have since learned that God answers prayers and that He will send angels as His messengers to answer those prayers and to fight to protect us in the heavenly places.[44]

WE HAVE NOT BECAUSE WE ASK NOT

I have previously touched on how limited my church and religious experiences were before I was twelve. I have mentioned my brief short-order requests of God, when I wanted Him to supply my needs or deliver me from my troubles. I easily turned to God in times of fear or tragedy: I ran to Him when my newborn baby's life was in jeopardy on the birthing table that early September morning in 1986. In trouble and completely helpless to change the situation, I cried aloud for God. At that time I had no relationship with God, but He knew me.

I was, however, quick to go back to my sinful ways for the eleven years between Marky's birth in 1986 and May 31, 1997, the day I accepted Jesus as my Lord and Savior. Soon thereafter my wife accepted Jesus, and so did all of my children. On October 7, 2000, a date that I will always cherish, Mark, Jr., forever placed his name into the Lamb's Book of Life.

Immediately after accepting Christ, I discontinued my "social work," my attempts to earn my way into heaven. Instead, when I went into those same streets, I had love to share and message to tell all who would listen. My newfound faith and the exciting truth about Jesus Christ filled the God-shaped void in my heart and in my life. That void I had tried to fill in so many different and disappointing ways was now forever and satisfyingly filled. I couldn't help but share this newfound answer that I had searched for all my life. My sins were forgiven and I was washed as white as snow. I was a new and different person, and I was excited about sharing the truth that had given me a new perspective on and energy for life. And I quickly realized that those people who hurt the most—those who knew heartache, pain, suffering, and poverty firsthand—were the first to receive and accept this good news of healing and hope.

I was on fire for God, I found His words in the Bible a source of life. I was a new creation in Christ (2 Corinthians 5:17), and I now understood what people meant when they talked about their personal relationship with Jesus. This experience was greater than any high, greater than any good time with the guys, and even greater than any relationship I had on this earth. Jesus was then—and is now—the foundation of my life. He is everything to me: the purpose for my life, the reason I get up in the morning, and the source of comfort and hope as I continue to deal with Marky's death.

I saw now that the days, months, and years I had studied, read, listened to, acted on, and lived out the Word of God had prepared me for the difficult challenges that were ahead for my family and me. I had failed to be the spiritual leader in my marriage and in my family until I understood that Jesus wanted to be my Lord. At that point and by the working of God's grace, I was taking on the God-assigned role that I was created for, and I was glad.

My desire to further my relationship with God consumed me, and the more I learned about my heavenly Father, the more I was in awe. God knew my name. God, the Creator of the universe knew me by name, and He knows you by name (John 10:3). And He knows the number of hairs on our heads (Mathew 10:30). More importantly, once we accept His Son as our Savior and Lord, God chooses to live within each of us: His indwelling Holy Spirit is our Guide, Comforter, and Teacher.

THE HOLY SPIRIT OF GOD

If you are have not yet accepted Jesus Christ as your Lord and Savior, that last statement may sound strange or even spooky. I will explain, but first I encourage you to ask God to reveal Himself to you, to help you learn about and understand His truth and love. He wants to help you see and accept His truth....

Most people accept the fact that we human beings are body, soul, and spirit. That being the case, our acceptance of Jesus as our Lord will impact our soul and our spirit. Now read this passage from Scripture asking God to help you understand it.

> *Now we have received, not the spirit of the world, but the Spirit who is from God, that we might know the things that have been freely given to us by God.*

These things we also speak, not in words which man's wisdom teaches but which the Holy Spirit teaches, comparing spiritual things with spiritual. But the natural man does not receive the things of the Spirit of God, for they are foolishness to him; nor can he know them, because they are spiritually discerned.

1 CORINTHIANS 2:12-14

God, our Creator, comes to live inside you and me when we choose to believe in His Son Jesus Christ. Here is Jesus' explanation of that gift:

If you love me, you will obey what I command. And I will ask the Father, and he will give you another Counselor to be with you forever— the Spirit of truth. The world cannot accept him, because it neither sees him nor knows him. But you know him, for he lives with you and will be in you.... Whoever has my commands and obeys them, he is the one who loves me. He who loves me will be loved by my Father, and I too will love him and show myself to him.

JOHN 14:15-17, 21 NIV

We need, however, to do more than acknowledge the validity of these facts about Jesus. We need to not only believe in God the Creator and Sustainer of the universe, but we also need to recognize that Jesus is His Son and that His death on the cross was God's plan to bridge the gap between sinful humanity and His own holiness. It is not enough to believe that God exists. As the apostle James pointed out, "even the demons believe that" (James 2:19), but that belief does not guarantee God's forgiveness of their rebellion or a place in heaven for eternity. A personal relationship with Jesus—what I saw in my mother-in-law and was so attracted to—is what changes both one's life on this earth and one's eternity.

MY EARLY YEARS IN CHRIST: 1997-2002

During my first five years as a Christian, other believers told me that they understood God's call on my life to be service as an "unconventional pastor" in an unconventional church—a church without walls—on the streets, in housing projects, and, today and as a result of Marky's passing, in public parks.

After I had shared God's truth on the streets and in the alleyways for several weeks, the Lord showed me that we needed a gathering place. The street mission I founded was called "Jesus Lives Ministries & Brighter Days Children's Mission." I leased a small building from which we started serving the poor, the homeless, and the children living in poverty. Within only six months, we went from serving food and offering clothing one day a week to being open seven days a week. We always served a hot meal on Sundays, and every Sunday afternoon I shared a message with the visitors. The attendance grew to over one hundred and fifty per week, with many people each week coming to recognize the truth about who Jesus is. We would serve food, offer clothing, and minister to whoever came through the doors.

A wonderful aspect of our ministry to the poor was our wagon ministry. We had six large Little Tikes wagons with "I love Jesus" and "Brighter Days Children's Mission" written on them. Young children living in poverty would come to our building, fill a wagon with food and clothing, and then pull the gifts home to their families, often with an adult being sure they got home safely. Those wagons were a witness to the neighborhood families that someone cared and that God loves them. Lives were changed for the good in Christ's name, and we had many joyful days as God used us to welcome people into His family. That ministry lasted for over five years, and those were blessed days.

In February 2000, Dena and I were blessed with our son Dominic. His name means "a gift from God" and "belonging to the Lord.". God knew on that day in 2000, when Dominic was born and Marky was thirteen, that in just five short years Marky would be going home to heaven....

In 2002, I knew it was time for me to move on from this street ministry. I had no idea what challenges lay just ahead for our family, but I was confident that it was time for me to close this chapter of my ministry life. I prayed diligently and waited—and waited—for God to provide someone to take over the mission. In the fall of 2002, a young woman named Gina Moon walked into the mission. She told me that the Lord sent her there, and she shared her vision for helping the homeless and the poor. The Word of Life Ministries was birthed that day, and some twelve years later the ministry continues to serve the lost, the hurting, and the poor—now from their new 18,000-square-foot building. God truly blessed and continues to bless this ministry to the lost, the hurting, and the poor.

Word of Life Street Ministry to the lost, hurting and poor in Barberton, Ohio "offering a hand up and not just a handout"—Gina Moon, Director (now located in a newly remodeled 18,000 sq. ft. building)

Sharing food and the Lord with "John" who was nestled among the homeless on the streets of New Orleans in 2009; In return . . . he blessed me with Godly words of wisdom

WALKING WITH JESUS: 2002-2006

The next four years of my life were a battleground marked by attacks from the enemy that seemed surreal....

In 2002, my family almost lost our then seven-year-old Brooke: a botched emergency appendectomy nearly cost her life. We took her from an Akron hospital and drove her to Pittsburgh, where God used doctors there to save her. Today Brooke is a healthy fourteen-year-old, and I thank God daily for her and for her total healing.

The strain of Brooke's illness, coupled with my failure to fully understand and obey God's instructions to husbands, opened a door into my family's life—and Satan burst through! An expert deceiver (John 8:44), Satan even used people in the church, especially a senior pastor, to do the most damage to my family. I started paying the price for some choices I had made before becoming a Christian and for failing to be a spiritual leader for my wife and family while we were on vacation in Pennsylvania on Easter Sunday 2003. But I'm getting ahead of myself....

I had dedicated my life to the Lord, and I had done everything I could think of to serve him. But my priorities were wrong. Miserably wrong. My wife and I were full-time parents, we were spending sixty hours a week running our real estate company, and we were directing a ministry that was open 365 days a year. We were going 24/7.

Unknowingly, I was failing to live according to God's priorities for His people. A godly husband and father puts God first and his spouse second, followed by his children, his job, and, if it is not his vocation, his ministry. In 2003, however, my mistaken order of priorities was God first and my children second, followed by my ministry and my job as real-estate broker and investor. My wife was at the end of the line. Consequently we were very vulnerable to the enemy's attacks—and attack he did.

16

The Battle on the Frontlines

It's not at all a secret. God's Word is very clear about the fact that Satan prowls around like a roaring lion looking to destroy people who have named Jesus their Savior and Lord (1 Peter 5:8). I knew that truth, I knew that I should put on my spiritual armor to protect myself, and I knew that every follower of Christ will encounter spiritual warfare. I faced it many times during the five years I served in the street ministry. The devil doesn't sit back when God's people are taking the gospel truth about Jesus to the middle of the devil's stomping grounds. Typically Satan uses his addictive weapons like crime, sexual abuse, drugs, and alcohol to maintain a strong hold on the downtrodden people living in poverty.

Jesus came to help the lost, hurting, and poor—not only those who are poor economically, but those who are poor in Spirit as well. When we start telling people that the way out of their difficulties is not a government program, the welfare system, drugs, or alcohol—that their way out and their only real hope is to turn to Jesus Christ—we need to be ready to rumble with the enemy. Like every Christian, I have had a target on my back for the enemy to shoot at since day one of my salvation, and the target is there to this day. Jesus Himself tells us that in this world we will have trouble (John 16:33), so we shouldn't be at all surprised.

But we Christ-followers serve the One who is mightier than the devil. I know what happens in the end: the devil and his demons burn in the lake of fire forever (Revelation 20:10). The devil can smell the sulfur burning, and he definitely knows that his days are numbered!

Back to my story… I knew what my priorities should be. I thought I was learning to deal with pride and an overzealous nature, both fueled by a well-entrenched and sinful sense of self-righteousness. I was a young Christian who had jumped immediately into street ministry when I still had much to learn about my faith. Oh, I was discipled along the way—I was learning at church from Pastor Mike, and I was studying men of God like Charles Stanley, Jack Graham, Billy Graham, Jentezen Franklin, and many others—but much of what I learned was in the school of hard knocks on the streets and in our ministry. My experience has taught me that a more effective and productive path would have included more discipleship before I stepped into ministry.

VITAL PARTS

So, in the fall of 2002, after Brooke's recovery, my wife and I were drained emotionally, financially, and spiritually. We were extremely vulnerable as a husband and wife, and our family was vulnerable as well, yet I thought everything was all right. Many times the man is the last to recognize and admit that his marriage is suffering or his wife is unhappy. And the deceiver capitalizes on that fact. I was deceived and about to face the biggest satanic encounter I had experienced up until that time.

I learned this truth after the fact—and I believe it was from a Jentezen Franklin broadcast: "If Satan cannot kill you, your witness, your ministry, or your testimony, he will attack your vital parts." In my case, the first attack was on my child Brooke; the enemy's next attacks would be on my wife, my marriage, my home; and, ultimately, the enemy attacked my son, my firstborn child, Mark Jr.

HOPE FOR SURVIVORS

The next few pages are very painful to write, yet very necessary to the story I'm telling. After much prayer and seeking the Lord for wisdom, guidance, and discernment, I am offering our testimony of the near destruction of our family. It is a major factor in Marky's passing—in his pain and heartache—and in the battle in the spiritual realm to kill and destroy me, my wife, and my family. My vital parts.

This subject is rarely discussed by Christians, and there seems to be a false belief that if the topic is ignored, it will go away. But according to the 2002 Southern Baptist Convention, "clergy sexual abuse (CSA) has reached horrific proportions in many churches today." This serious problem is not limited to any one denomination; it can be found among church leaders throughout the Christian community. Its occurrence surely grieves God, and the enemy seizes each incident as a tool of destruction that works from within the body of Christ. (You can read more about CSA in appendix B, "The Devastating Epidemic of Clergy Abuse.")

A WOLF IN SHEPHERD'S CLOTHING

On Easter Sunday 2003, while on vacation in Pennsylvania, my family was about to fall victim to the adulterous pastor who, for more than fifteen years, had preyed upon innocent women, vulnerable marriages, and the weakened families that result when marriages falter. This abusive pastor was a trusted senior pastor at a major Cleveland, Ohio, area church, but his traveling allowed him to leave a path of destruction all over Ohio and throughout the country.

This wolf in shepherd's clothing was well equipped with degrees in theology, psychology, and marriage counseling. For years, he used his education, position, and charm to gain the trust of vulnerable women in troubled marriages. Ironically, in addition to his church salary, he earned extra income counseling unsuspecting couples at local marriage retreats. And his wife led those with him.

This man had a cultlike following supported by board members he himself had appointed, men who have been quoted as saying they would die for this pastor. One of his board members said on numerous occasions that he "felt like taking his shoes off in his presence because the pastor is so holy." This so-called man of God secretly manipulated his way into my marriage and, over a one-year period, nearly destroyed my family. Predators like him who gain people's trust in the name of God and then violate that trust are the worst kind of hypocrite in the church, and many women and families are their victims.

But Dena and I made public our experience. Over a two-week period in the fall of 2003, our family—along with our pastor—brought to the violating pastor's church documented evidence of his CSA. We shared the truth first with the church's board of elders and then with the church body. The pastor and his cohorts did not leave without a fight. The predatory senior pastor was ultimately fired from his position, and the board was systematically dismantled. His fifteen-year reign of abuse ended, much to his dismay. Several more victims and their families stepped forward soon after my family and I did.

DEVASTATION SPIRITUAL AND EMOTIONAL

Victims of any type of abuse want three things: the truth told, the abuse to stop for themselves and others, and a policy put in place for it to never happen again.

The abuse we as a family suffered at the hands of this pastor and his church leaders was devastating. Each one of us was severely wounded emotionally and spiritually. But God saw us through that two-year nightmare, which—from my perspective—culminated in Marky's passing that July 2005 morning. Mark, Jr., never fully recovered from the abuse.

Marky was a wounded child: both a victim and a witness to the worst type of abuse imaginable—the abuse, devastation, and near destruction of the family he loved. Prior to this attack on our family in 2003, Marky was a B student and a phenomenal athlete who was never in any serious trouble. But in 2004 he was hurting—as we all were. What role did the abuse of my wife, Marky, our marriage, and our family play in Marky's death? God only knows....

If you are a victim of CSA or were ever hurt by a church, directly or indirectly, please hear me: you cannot afford to make a decision that will impact your eternal future based on your hurt or on the hypocrisy of sinful human beings. Read that again: you cannot afford to make a decision that will impact your eternal future based on your hurt or on the hypocrisy of sinful human beings.

MAN'S PLAN AND AGENDA VS. GOD'S PLAN

So I plead with you to get a Bible and learn about Jesus. Read the Gospels of Matthew, Mark, Luke, and John and let God's Spirit help you see Jesus correctly. Again, don't let the hurt you've experienced as a result of man's deception keep you from discovering for yourself who the real Jesus Christ truly is. And as you get to know about Him, you will see that no one has ever been hurt or betrayed in a worse manner by the church—by the religious people of the day—than Jesus Christ Himself. He understands your disillusionment with the institutional church. May that truth encourage you as you get to know Jesus. After all, your eternal future depends on your knowing and accepting the truth about who Jesus truly is—and on knowing Him personally as Savior and Lord.

It is no wonder that many people run from "church" as they know it. I myself ran from what I thought the church was for thirty-nine years, until that day 1997 when I met a true man of God feeding the poor in the housing projects. Then I read about Jesus' life and was forever changed.[45]

A FRESH START AND FORGIVENESS

Since 2008, we have been blessed to be in a church here in Florida that has a godly pastor, church leaders of integrity, and church members who wholeheartedly serve, love, and honor God. Good churches do exist.

For me, life without Jesus Christ is unimaginable. I have experienced life without hope, but I know that no matter what in life's circumstances that takes place, God is our refuge and our hope if we allow Him to be.

And turning to God like that is hard to do, if not impossible, if we let unforgiveness and bitterness take root in our lives. The lack of forgiveness is a poison that slowly contaminates and ultimately destroys our spirit and soul. Good and evil cannot occupy our mind, heart, and soul at the same time. Either we forgive or we are bitter. I knew I had to forgive the church and our abusers, but that commandment from the Lord—given for our good—is difficult to obey. Someone much wiser than I told me to pray as Jesus did on the cross: "Father God, forgive them for they do not know what they are doing." So I asked God to forgive my abusers when I could not forgive them on my own.

Finally, in 2008, three years after the horrible deeds had been done, I was able to forgive—within my heart—all of the abusers who had inflicted hurt and pain on my wife, my son, my family, and me. I gave all the pain, bitterness, resentment, and, most importantly, unforgiveness over to God.

As any painful experience in life, though, this lack of forgiveness tries to creep back into my life from time to time. When it does, I counter those feelings with truths from the Bible, truths often expressed in praise music that fills one's mind, heart, and soul with truth and goodness. God's Word brings hope and healing after the darkest kinds of devastation.

17

Our Redeemer God... Very Much at Work

So what is our healing and redeemer God doing in the lives of the Canfora family now? The same kind of things He wants to do in your life.

TIMMY'S DAD

Recently, when I was leaving a real estate office here in Panama City, I held open the front door for a sixty-three-year-old man who two years earlier had a stroke that left him partially paralyzed. He entered the office ever so slowly, and I encouraged him to take his time. The friend who was with him kindly thanked me as we both helped him to his seat in the lobby. Before I headed to the parking lot, though, I knew that God wanted me to take a minute and talk with this man. Having learned again and again the importance of obeying such nudges from the Lord, I walked back into the lobby and sat down.

The man looked at me with empty eyes, and his expression was painful to see. Just looking into his eyes nearly brought me to tears. Due to his tattered life, he looked much, much older than his sixty-three years. I made small talk, and he nodded politely. I then asked him what had happened. In his slow, methodical, yet slurred speech, he explained that he had had a stroke two years ago.

At that point I asked if he knew the Lord, and he slowly shook his head no. Then I gently said, "If you had passed away when you had the stroke, do you know where you would have spent eternity?"

Ever so slowly, he shook his head no, and this time a tear rolled down his cheek. My heart broke for him, and I could barely speak. I gently told him about Jesus and the love and forgiveness we can find in Him. I told my new friend that he was just one simple prayer away from guaranteeing himself a place in heaven: he needed only to acknowledge that Jesus is God's Son and welcome Him as his Lord and Savior. With that heartfelt prayer, by accepting Jesus' death on behalf of his sins and Jesus' resurrection as victory over that sin, this man would know new life on earth and eternal life in heaven. I told him if he prayed that prayer and meant it, he would go to heaven when he died. I held his hand as we prayed together, and tears rolled down our both of our cheeks.

His friend returned to the lobby in the middle of our prayer, and she stood there in silence. Tears formed in her eyes, too. After I finished praying, she said that she was a Christian and explained that this man had had a child named Timmy. Several years earlier, when he was only eleven, Timmy had passed away. Living with that great pain, this man had never been the same after his son's death.

That was when I told the two of them about Marky and how sure I was that, at that very moment, Marky and Timmy were rejoicing together in heaven, rejoicing that now Timmy's daddy would be in heaven in God's perfect time....

This is how God works. I've experienced it again and again, whenever I've obeyed His gentle prompting. He takes a simple gesture of kindness—holding open a door for a hurting man—and saves that person's soul.

SIX ALABAMA YOUTHS

One day when Dominic and I were at the baseball batting cages in Panama City Beach, I noticed six young black men ranging in ages from eighteen to twenty-two standing around the fast-pitch machine. They all were dressed in their baggy pants, half-tilted ball caps, chains, and gear. Many of today's youth call themselves Bangers (short for "gang bangers"), thugs, or gangstas, and the media have labeled them Generation Next.

As I approached them—at the Lord's prompting—I knew I was going to have some fun. I always try to break the ice with a little humor, and this time I said something like this: "What's up, fellas? What do you say we see who is the best hitter here. I'll put my son Dominic up against your best hitter. Let's see what you got!"

I was straight faced, but laughing inside as eight-year-old Dominic stood next to me with his baseball bat in hand. He loves it when I banter with kids.

One young man responded quickly: "All right, man, what do you want to hit for $20?"

I quickly responded, "No, we are playing for something greater than twenty bucks! We're playing for the championship of Panama City Beach. For braggin' rights."

Now the seriousness was gone, and we all started laughing. We hit baseballs in the cages together, Dom's game was on, and the guys immediately took a liking to him. They really were cool kids, too, but if looks could kill, these guys would have been on death row.

While I was standing there waiting on the Lord, one of the young men who had been looking at the ministry T-shirt I was wearing came up to me and said, "What's that, man, 'A Celebration of Life'?"

Bingo! I thought. *Here we go, Lord. An open door.*

I told him about Marky's life, and he immediately shared with me that his fourteen-year-old sister had passed away a year ago. While swimming, she had had an epileptic seizure and drowned... as her father sat on the shore. As he spoke, this young man's tough façade dissolved in his inaudible words of pain and heartache as he tried to fight back the tears.

I quickly told him that his sister had gone instantly into the arms of Jesus when she passed away and that she was alive and doing well in heaven. After all, she had a new body and no more seizures or pain. Her brother's sagging head lifted and our eyes met. I further explained his sister's desire for him to join her there one day.

The father in me quickly felt the pain his dad undoubtedly feels, the dad who was right there while his baby drowned. I also knew from experience how the devil—the enemy—torments with false guilt the loved ones, friends, siblings, and parents of a child who passes. But even as Satan accuses, Jesus intercedes (Zechariah 3:1; Hebrews 7:25).

As I put my hand on this young man's shoulder and looked into his tear-filled eyes, I asked, "Do your mom and dad know the Lord?"

He replied, "My mom does, and she's doing all right, I guess. But not my dad. It's killing him."

That's when I interrupted and asked, "Is it drugs or alcohol or both that he uses to try to kill the pain?"

He replied, "Both, sir, and it's killing him."

By this time the other five young men and my Dominic were standing with us. I quickly explained that both Marky and this young man's sister were in heaven. I then said, "Are we all right? Am I all right with you fellas?"

"Oh yeah, man. You are all right with us," they replied.

"Then will you please give me a few minutes to talk to you? Have a seat here on the bleachers. If you don't like what I have to say, you can go. It was a good time, and we had fun." By this time, several other people on this very busy street near the beach had overheard and were listening from afar.

I proceeded to talk about the love of Christ, eternity in heaven, and the hope and healing the Jesus Christ offers everyone. Fifteen minutes later, these young men gathered in a circle, held hands, and closed their eyes. Dominic started our prayer—"Dear Jesus, thank You for this day"— and I finished it. All six accepted Christ: their afternoon spent hitting a baseball had moved them from utter darkness and hopelessness to light and hope in Jesus. Despite the rush of the cars passing by and the curious people watching, God heard the prayer and had moved in the lives of these, His precious children.

We parted with hugs and high fives, and they promised me they would share this message of hope with the young man's mom and dad. They had a hometown church to go to, the one the young man's mom attended, and they assured me that they would follow God for the rest of their lives. I pray for them regularly and trust them to the good Lord's care.

EASTER SUNDAY 2008

The developer I worked for in Florida and his family were in town for spring break. On Easter Sunday Dena and I had all the staff, some friends, and their families over for a picnic, about seventy-five people in all, including twenty-five children. As the day wore on, the neighbor who lived behind my home on the second floor of a two-story building was yelling loudly out his window at our group. I first thought our music was too loud or, since it had a Christian message, was perhaps offensive to him.

But this extremely large man, leaning over the railing of his balcony just above our picnic area, was bellowing out some very harsh expletives. His son and his wife, who was a good foot and a half shorter than her husband's 6'4", 380-pound frame, stood next to him. The man—whose name I learned later was Chris—was visibly upset, and he was directing most of his insults at a particular couple. When I saw whom Chris was addressing, I thought he might actually have a legitimate complaint: I was well aware of many underhanded things this couple had done in the past. In fact, they were also known to be pathological liars. This couple had, for instance, recently warned me about Chris, saying that he was a skin-headed Nazi with a swastika on his neck and an extremely dangerous drug abuser who had threatened their lives. I didn't exactly trust the source of this information, and I was eager to hear this towering, giant-of-a-man's side of things.

As I prayed—and I started to immediately when the yelling began again—the Lord helped me see Chris as one of God's hurting children. Then I sensed the Lord saying, *Invite him to the party, but first take them some food and soft drinks.* As I loaded several plates with all the food I could fit on them, the woman who had told me about this neighbor was getting nervous.

"What are you doing?" she exclaimed.

"Taking my neighbors some food. It was rude of us not to invite them," I said matter-of-factly. Her obvious nervousness spoke volumes to me, and I knew I was on the right path.

"But he'll hurt you! He's dangerous and crazy!"

As I looked at her, she babbled on more and more, and I became increasingly confident that the Lord was nudging me to visit my neighbors. I grabbed the plates and drinks and headed toward the staircase leading up to Chris's balcony. Praying under my breath as I approached, I looked at this very large and angry man and thought, *Wow, Lord! He looks a lot like Goliath must have looked to David.* And that balcony added another fifteen feet to his height! The difference between Goliath and this man was key, though: Goliath was guilty of mocking God and deserved his fate, but I would soon find out that Chris was innocent of any crime. As I got closer to him, he looked down at me and said for everyone to hear, "If you are a friend of theirs, do not come near my home."

I continued up the stairs and said, "I just want to bring you some food and talk with you for a minute." When these words left my mouth, I was halfway up the stairs. And at that point Chris took his fist—that was as large as a small basketball—and punched his gas barbecue. It tumbled backward and fell loudly onto the floor of the balcony. I kept walking, admittedly a bit slower, and said as I reached the top step, "I am here for the truth. I want to hear your side." Hearing those few words, Chris stopped dancing in his boxing position and lowered his fists.

I quickly told him and his wife that I was a man of God and a person of integrity, that I wanted the truth told, and that I would gladly listen to them. As they simultaneously told me all the false accusations, I gently asked if we could go inside, explaining that I would hear them out at their kitchen table. As I entered their home, I was aware that the entire group below was standing in silence. The only people stirring were the false accusers, and they were uneasy to say the least.

As I sat in the kitchen table, I learned that the accusing couple had stolen this family's paid rent money for over six months; the couple at my party had not turned in the money to the landlord. Then, when confronted by the property owner, the thieves' reaction was to try to discredit the renters—when they were in the middle of an investigation and at risk of losing custody of their nine-year-old child. Furthermore, Chris and his wife had been falsely accused of drug use, child endangering, and other claims that were later dismissed by the authorities.

I let these two people speak, and then I shared my testimony. It turned out their nine-year-old son had had major brain surgery when he was just two years old. Seeing that they dearly loved this boy, I explained to them how much God, their heavenly Father, loved them; how God had given them these precious seven years with their son; and that he was standing there with us because God loved them and was continuing to bless them. Then both parents began to cry uncontrollably.

That was when this Goliath of a man brought out newspaper clippings from Chicago: at nine years old, Chris had watched and intervened as his mom was brutally raped by a black man; later, when he was fourteen, she was murdered. This was the root of his pain, his racism, and his anger. When Chris said that his mom believed in Jesus, I explained salvation to him and told him of his mother's desire from heaven for him and his family to come to the Lord and ultimately join her one day in heaven. That very night, at that kitchen table, the father, mother, and son welcomed Jesus as their Savior and Lord.

A few moments later, my friend Nathan knocked on the door to see if I was all right because I had been gone so long. The Easter gathering was now over, and the sun was setting. As we walked back to the house, he showed me the gun he had in his pocket. With a laugh he said, "I thought maybe he had killed you up there."

I joked back, "Well, if he had, you only showed up about an hour too late."

Our ministry later took the family an adult Bible, a children's Bible, and the Bible on CD for his wife doesn't like to read. Chris and I are friends to this day, and the false charges made against them were later dropped.

ONE THOUSAND KIDS, ONE THOUSAND FAMILIES

Every spring and summer at Frank Brown Park here in Panama City Beach, Florida, the city sponsors one of the largest children's baseball tournaments in the nation. In 2009 God nudged me to pass out our *Read and Believe* ministry baseball poster to each child and every family attending that three-day event.

By the way, you may be wondering how I distinguish between a nudge from God and a half-baked Mark idea. My rule of thumb is this: *Would God want me to do this—and does it glorify Jesus Christ?* Or, approached differently, *Would Satan be prompting me to offer hope in the name of Christ?* In many cases, the answers to these questions are obvious.

Since I was coaching Dominic's team at the tournament, I had to be at Frank Brown Park anyway. So in between our games, Dominic and I handed out the "I can do all things through Christ" Philippians 4:13 baseball posters to the families in the stands. In all, the ninety-six teams in the tournament meant a thousand or more players, ranging in age from five to sixteen and coming from ten different states. Between innings of the various games, I began to share briefly about the photo, Marky, and the history of the ministry. It wasn't long before I had the attention of everyone in the bleachers, and several families from that single team had had a child pass away or knew of a family that had experienced the passing of a child. Their response to what I shared was gracious, loving, and kind. I prayed with many families and was asked to speak to some teams about drug abuse, children loving their parents, and parents loving their children right where they are.

By the final day of the tournament, I had prayed with several hurting parents, talked to many children about Marky and Jesus, and handed out one thousand posters that now adorn bedroom walls in ten states. I was

Dominic holding one of our Read and Believe Ministry baseball posters
(Get yours free at our ministry web site: www.IveGotHope.com)

blessed beyond measure.

One mother came up to me at the end of the tournament and, pointing to a father standing by the backstop, said, "You see that dad? After you spoke to us yesterday, he apologized to all of us parents for how he has mistreated his twelve-year-old son during the season with his verbal outbursts and public criticism. He went on to say that he had heard you, a man who has lost your son and had come to us to share from your heart and remind us of the precious gift we have in our kids and what you would give for just one more day or hour here on this earth with your son. That dad humbly said he will never again speak harshly to his son, and he apologized to us one more time."

GOD'S REDEMPTIVE POWER

Maybe you've heard it said that nothing—no loss, no tragedy, no pain—is beyond the reach of God's redemptive power. I can attest to the amazing truth of that statement. Truly, absolutely no hurtful experience we face is beyond His redemptive power and work. He truly does bring good out of the seemingly pointless tragedy. Timmy's dad, the six Alabama youth, Chris and his family, and the reformed baseball dad are just a few examples of what God has done through us since Marky went home to be with Him.

Whatever your story—whatever pain you have experienced—God wants to show you His redemptive power. So my prayer for you is that you will have eyes that see as God's children the people He puts in your path, a heart that is soft toward them, and a God-based courage to listen and talk with those people. Each of us has a story… and each of us needs to hear the story of God's hope, the story of Jesus Christ.

18

Lessons Learned

Have you learned some of life's most valuable lessons the hard way? More often than any of us would like to admit, that's the case. And, I believe, that is evidence of God's redemptive touch on those hard ways that do indeed teach us important truths. Allow me to humbly share some of what I've learned since Marky passed....

LOVE YOUR KIDS RIGHT WHERE THEY ARE

One of God's great works in my life has been—as I've mentioned throughout these pages—to reinforce what a blessing our kids are and how we are to love our children our children as God loves us: unconditionally, no matter what, and right where they are. That truth bears repeating: God accepts us right where we are and right along with the messes we have made and the mess we are currently in. God loves you and me unconditionally. We don't have to get the sin completely out of our lives before we can receive the love and saving grace God offers us. He wants you and me to go to Him just as we are. God already has forgiven us, through Jesus' death on the cross, for all our sin—past, present, and future. None of us can ever be good enough or do enough good things to earn God's love and entrance into heaven. Only by our faith in the sufficiency of God's grace and mercy, shown us in the death and resurrection of His Son Jesus, can we truly experience God's love and forgiveness. We simply must accept that free gift.

Yes, God loves us just as we are, and we are to love our children the exact same way... unconditionally... and right where they are.

WORDS OF HOPE

• **About stumbling** — Since Marky's passing, I have stumbled thousands of times. I have doubted God's plan for my life a thousand times. I have asked God "Why?" a thousand times. I have wrestled with bitterness a thousand times. And I have cried countless times. Thousands of times in the last four years I have strayed from God's path of hope and healing. I would be remiss, a hypocrite, and a liar if I spoke only of my victories. As many of you know from a loss of your own, especially in the early days and months the smallest remembrance of the loved one who has passed can trigger profound, intense, deep, and excruciating feelings of pain and loneliness.

Even now, when I doubt, I try to immediately recall past victories and the promises of our ever-faithful God.... When I ask God "Why?" I remember that He let His Son Jesus suffer and die for us on that cross.... When I am bitter, I think of the many lives God has changed for the good by using my message about Marky's life.... And when I cry, I cry. I let it all out. A good cry is therapeutic and healing. And then I spend time focusing on the promises of God.

• **About turning to God for strength** — Has life ever forced you to consider how you're doing on your own, apart from God? Each of us approaches every new day in our own way, and whether or not we know Jesus makes a difference.

Every morning, for instance, when I roll out of my bed, I fall directly to my knees and simply ask God to be my strength for that day. A young man here in Florida told me, "Hey, Mr. Mark, I tried that rollin' to my knees and talkin' to God in the mornings. It really helped me a lot. Thanks."

One day at a time, God is our strength. One day at a time, God will be our strength... *if we choose to allow Him to be.*

I also find strength in the appendix D "God's Promises About Our Children and Loved Ones in Heaven." (You can print that list from our Web site www.IveGotHope.com.)

Your way of finding strength may be unique to you. You may also learn from how others find strength for tough times. Whatever ways you choose, let God be the focus, and He will, moment by moment, give you the strength that you need for whatever you face.

• **About choosing to do the right thing** — When we put our trust in God and do what He commands us to do, we will always find the results of our obedience infinitely greater than we could have ever imagined. To be sure, it can be very hard to do the right thing, but obedience to God's ways leads to life more abundantly as we experience His pleasure in us and as He uses our obedience to bring blessings to others. You see, it truly is better to give than to receive. When we serve God and when we serve others, we ourselves are blessed beyond measure. And when we live in obedience to God's will for our lives—when we reach out to others in love and see God set them free in Christ—words cannot convey the hope, peace, and joy we experience. (One easy way to share hope is to give a copy of this book to someone who is hurting. Ask God to use His truth within these covers to heal that person's broken heart and to bring hope where there is hopelessness.).

And that hope, peace, and joy we experience when we obey God stand in sharp contrast to what happens when we choose to do the wrong thing, when we are involved in alcohol, drugs, affairs, stealing, lying, cheating—and the grim list goes on and on. In the beginning, our sin of choice can feel pretty good, but that lasts only for a moment. The lie people buy into—the lie from the deceiver, the lie straight from the pit of hell—is that sin brings pleasure. Ultimately and always, in each and every case, the wrong action goes from causing good feelings to causing pain, heartache, misery, addiction, humiliation, the loss of family or friends, and, many times, death. And death before we're reconciled with God—death that will mean eternal separation from Him—is Satan's goal for all of us.

Doing the right thing is hard at the beginning, but it leads to life. Doing the wrong thing is alluring and attractive at the beginning, and it always and eventually leads to misery and death.

• **About the blame game: don't play it!** — One of the worst consequences of a child or loved one's passing is the "blame game" that too often results—and it is hardly a game. Blaming someone for something that was totally beyond his or her control—for instance, the number of days God granted a loved one to live on this earth—hurts the accuser as well as the accused. No wonder blame is one of the enemy's prime weapons. This wrong act of pointing the finger only furthers the pain and suffering of everyone touched by the loss.

Not only does Satan use people to accuse each other, but he accuses us too. He puts in our minds wrong ideas about our loved one's death, and we must respond with the truth that God gives us the days we live, that He has numbered since before the world began the days each and every one of us would spend on this earth.

In the aftermath of a loved one's passing, we may find it easier to choose to accuse rather than cling to God and His truth. Arguing can result, more strife can be added, and more afflictions heaped on top of an already unbearable and unimaginable pain—and all of this taking place while that child or loved one is at peace, comforted with a new body, and living the best life imaginable in heaven. The one who passed has gone from life on earth to abundant life in heaven.

So, if you have been caught in the blame game—either receiving or giving blame—forgive that person or forgive yourself, and you both will be set free. Don't let bitterness rule and ruin your life. Forgiveness is a major step on the healing journey.

A NEW AND BRIGHTER DAY

In the spring of 2008, I had a dream a few hours after I watched the news story about an eighteen-year-old University of Alabama student who was raped and nearly murdered during the annual college spring break party here in Panama City Beach. After being viciously assaulted at the hotel where she was staying, she was thrown from the sixth floor of the building. Thank God her fall was slowed when she hit a lower stairwell landing, and she miraculously survived that attempted murder.

Through this dream, God motivated me to try to end this abuse. Once again He woke me in the middle of the night and, while drawing a huge line in the sand from the Gulf of Mexico waters to a high-rise tower, cried, "No more!!!" Then in His small voice He asked me, *What if that were your daughter? She* is *My daughter.*

As I lay in bed weeping for that young woman, I asked God to forgive me for initially being so unmoved by the news of such a horrific tragedy. Immediately I went to my computer to start acting in obedience to God's nudge.

After days of extensive research, I was shocked and horrified to discover that Panama City Beach has been the site of thousands of rapes, assaults, and numerous deaths over the years, including the 2005 murder of a local police officer on Easter Sunday. Each year, for three to four weeks straight, this gathering—the nation's largest gathering of college students—made Panama City Beach a war zone as ambulances, fire engines, EMS workers, police, and hospitals were overwhelmed 24/7 by college students who made wrong choices, often falling victim to criminals and sexual predators.

Each year MTV and one-hundred-thousand-plus students have gathered here to "party." Many of these young people who came with hopes and dreams of fun and excitement were, tragically, sent home in body bags. Many more students leave wounded, severely injured, battered, and scarred emotionally if not physically for life. Countless thousands of students and their families have suffered from the tragic results of this annual tradition, results that had for too long gone virtually ignored by the local churches and quietly tolerated by community members. Many locals felt hopeless; most locals had become numb to the violence.

So, acting on God's nudge, I founded Families & Friends for a Safe Panama City Beach and organized a fifteen-month-long effort to reveal the tragic truths about this annual event. We brought together business leaders, professionals, teachers, doctors, retired police, EMS workers, churches, students, and youth groups that united to put an end to spring break as it had always been observed.

Now that the truth has been brought to light, local authorities are moving toward making Panama City Beach a family-friendly destination. For the first time in twenty-five years, for instance, the local Tourist Development Council declared it would no longer finance college spring break: MTV would no longer receive the community's money to throw a party that has hurt so many. The city is also scheduling weeks for safe, family-friendly vacations each year around Easter Sunday. The city's beaches are among the country's most beautiful and should be enjoyed by everyone. This effort to help families and to protect college students marked a major turning point in my healing process, and it all occurred as I was drafting much of this book. (You can get more information on this ongoing effort at www.SafePCB.com. Also, the Billy Graham Crusade will be partnering with us for a "Rock the Beach" festival in the spring of 2011.)

THE LORD KEEPS NUDGING

The Canfora family has lived in Florida for three years now, and God continues to use our ministry in Ohio, Florida, Georgia, Alabama, and much of the Southeastern United States. On Easter weekend, April

11, 2009, for instance, we had our first annual "Celebration of Life and Family" festival in Panama City Beach. This was an effort to bring people together during spring break to celebrate the precious gift of life. As with all our events, everything is given out at no charge and in Jesus' name. Two thousand free ministry T-shirts (Marky's shirt ministry lives on!), thousands of Philippians 4:13 baseball posters, and lots of food were shared. Nine bands performed, including SM Souljah and number one Christian recording artist Lecrae. We then held our fourth annual Edgewood Park "Celebration of Life" festival in Barberton, Ohio, on July 11, 2009. At both events, thousands attended, and hundreds accepted Jesus as Lord and Savior when, at both events, the message of hope in Jesus Christ was shared.

Not too long before the Edgewood Park event, Dave—the man I met in the park's pavilion on the morning of Marky's passing (see chapter 5)—came across the street to help me prepare the festival signs. As we were finishing up in the parking lot, I sensed another one of those nudges from the Lord: *I'm not done with Dave yet. Ask him if he is saved, if he knows where he will spend eternity when he dies.*

So I turned to Dave and simply asked, "Can I ask you a question?" When he said yes, I continued: "Do you know where you will spend eternity when you die?" He slowly shook his head no as he shrugged his shoulders. "Have you ever accepted Jesus as Lord and Savior?" After a brief moment, he again shook his head no.

I said, "Do you want to pray with me and accept Jesus as your Lord and Savior?" That was when he nodded yes. We prayed and then hugged each other as tears filled our eyes. Four years had passed since that fateful morning when we met, and now we could see God's purpose more clearly and celebrate His blessing on this friendship.

When we step out in faith—in obedience to God's nudging—He always has for us something infinitely greater than we could ever have asked for or imagined. He ordains our meetings, those times when our path crosses another's path. We simply have to listen for and then obey His promptings, those nudges to do His will.

In this case, I thought I was simply getting signs ready for the festival. Dave thought he was being a good neighbor and helpful friend. But God had Dave's spirit, soul, and eternal future in mind, and God had planned this particular meeting since the beginning of time. Nothing that happens in your life or mine takes God by surprise. After all—and

Dave and Mark at Pavilion 2009

may we never stop marveling over this truth—He knows your name, He numbers the hair on your head, and He chooses to dwell inside of you if you choose to let Him.

THE LOVE OF GOD

Dave's salvation is a miracle, and such movement of God—in line with the truths of Romans 8:28 and Isaiah 61—fuels our "Celebration of Life and Message of Hope in Jesus Christ!" God's answers to the prayerful cries of this father prompt the heartfelt celebration of the gift of life on earth, our salvation, our new life in Christ, and our God-promised eternal life in heaven forever and ever and ever! We must walk through this life choosing to trust that God and His plans for us are good. I know that, through this—from my perspective—premature and therefore tragic passing of Marky, I have learned to trust more in the love of Jesus Christ. Now I am privileged to share His love with others, often by just listening to them talk about their pain.

God never promised that our time on this earth would be easy. In fact, as I've pointed out before, Jesus promises the exact opposite (John 16:33). But God has promised that He will never leave us nor forsake us; He will never let us go through our trials and hardships alone. In keeping His promise to never forsake us, God continues to answer us whenever we cry out to Him. He has faithfully answered the cries of this desperate and heartbroken father, and He will answer your cries as well.

Thank You, Lord! And to You and You alone be the glory!

SHARING GOD'S LOVE

You can share the love of God with others by supporting our ministry efforts to share this message of hope and healing in Jesus Christ. Whether you purchase a poster, T-shirt, book, or CD, whether you attend a meeting, gathering, or festival, your act of love will make you a part of God's work in the lives of hurting people. I have learned firsthand that God will use your giving to others when you are hurting to heal your soul. Even knowing that, I find it difficult to ask you to give. I am all too aware of the hypocrisy and poor use of people's donations all too common in ministries. But I will be brutally honest here: as I write, we are still paying off the two 2009 festivals. I am just communicating, though. I'm not worrying because I know God always provides.

Mark Canfora Ministries Presents...

A Celebration of Life & Family
Festival 2009
Panama City Beach
Pier Park Amphitheater
Easter Weekend
Saturday April 11, 2009
Cost: Free (Donations accepted at the event)

- Family Fun: Food • Games • Prizes • DJ: 1pm-4pm
- Concert: Live Music 4pm-9pm
- Bring your chairs and blankets...
- Come early...seating arrangements on a first come first serve basis.

Feature Artist: Lecrae

Mark & Dena Canfora

Jonathan Brewster aka "SMSouljah"

- **Feature Artist: Lecrae**
- **Jonathan Brewster aka "SMSouljah"**
- **Worship Artist: Dena Canfora**
- **Plus Other Local & Regional Bands**

Hip Hop University   Lil Royalty   Worship Team

For More Info Go To...
www.IveGotHope.com

S.A.L.T.
EYES EAST

#1 Recording Artist "Lecrae" lifting up the name of Jesus to thousands that attended our free Celebration of Life & Family Fest 2009, Panama City Beach, Florida

And believers were increasingly added to the Lord, multitudes of men, women, and children . . . Acts 5:14

(Clockwise from top left): Juliana, Mark Sr., Dominic, Lecrae, Dena, and Brooke, Celebration of Life & Family Fest, Panama City Beach, Florida 2009; My wife Dena at the Florida Fest 2009; A message of hope and healing, Mark Canfora, Florida Fest 2009

(Left): Mark Jr.'s friends/siblings gather after the funeral . . . Edgewood Park Barberton, Ohio, July 2005

(Below): SM Souljah with Dominic on stage "droppin' rhymes for the one (Jesus) that gave His life, yo" Edgewood Park Celebration of Life 2007

(Left): Mark Jr., Carly, Brooke, Juliana, and Dominic; May 2005 (last photo taken of my five children together)

(Below): Carly, Juliana, Brooke, and Dominic, Christmas 2009

(Left): Dena and I just recently celebrated our 15 year anniversary in 2009

(Below): Christmas 2009

FOUR WAYS YOU CAN HELP

I know not everyone is able to go out into the streets, parks, baseball fields, and street missions, but you can support those of us who can and do. Such support is as essential to this ministry as those who do the physical work and minister directly.

• **Donate to our Hope and Healing ministry efforts.** Posters, T-shirts, online books, music, festivals—all offering hope and healing—are shared at no cost and given in Jesus' name through our *Read and Believe* department. These outreach efforts to people who are suffering and in pain all cost us money.

• **Buy several books on audio and in print.** Give this gift of hope to the brokenhearted. We offer quantity discounts for books you can give to your church, youth group, and people you know who have suffered the passing of a loved one or child. You can also purchase books for us to give away at festivals, street missions, to newly grieving parents and families, etc.

• **Host your own Celebration of Life and Message of Hope festival.** We are willing and able to assist you in your efforts to organize and host your own gathering. We can email you an event director's template and guide that covers everything from stage, sound, and music to food, marketing, and an altar call that invites people to accept Jesus Christ as their Lord and Savior.

• **Prayer.** We need your prayers. Please forward news about our ministry to prayer chains—and please pray for every person, whether parent, sibling, other relative, or friend, who has already or who sometime will suffer the passing of a loved one. Please pray that these hurting people will come to know the healing and saving power of our Lord Jesus Christ.

I pray that if you have been helped or encouraged in any way by this book, you will become a part of this ongoing effort to help others.

In the love of Christ,
Mark Canfora
2433 Thomas Drive #125
Panama City Beach, Florida 32408
(330) 865-1000

For more information about books, T-shirts, baseball posters, and becoming a monthly partner, contact our Web site at www.IveGotHope.com or e-mail me at MarkCanfora@aol.com.

Those that sow in tears shall reap in joy. — Psalm 126:5

Find more festival photos, radio interviews, video footage, and testimonials at www.IveGotHope.com.

APPENDIX A

Truth for My Journey — and Yours

The words I share below are lifeblood to me, and they may be to you one day if they haven't been or aren't already. These are the words of truth and hope that God used to enable me to keep putting one foot in front of the other, and He will do the same for you, whatever valley you are walking through.

1. God knows the end from the beginning and the beginning from the end. God really knows all—past, present, and future. (Book Page 24)

   Why, you do not even know what will happen tomorrow. What is your life? You are a mist that appears for a little while and then vanishes. Instead, you ought to say, "If it is the Lord's will, we will live and do this or that."
   JAMES 4:14-15 NIV

2. Sooner or later, everyone experiences death—the death of a friend, a family member, and inevitably his or her own death. On that day of accountability, each and every one of us will stand before God and face the truth of who He is, what He has required of us, and how far short of His standards we have fallen. (Book Page 24)

   "As surely as I live," says the Lord, "every knee will bow before me; every tongue will confess to God." So then, each of us will give an account of himself to God.
   ROMANS 14:11-12

3. God knit us together in our mother's womb, and He knows the day we will be born and the day we will die. (Book Page 25)

What will I do when God confronts me?
What will I answer when called to account?

Did not he who made me in the womb make them?
Did not the same one form us both within our mothers?
    JOB 31:14-16

4. For those of us who believe that Jesus is God's Son and have accepted him as our Lord and Savior, God promises everlasting life in heaven with our children who pass on before us. (Book Page 29)

For God so loved the world that He gave His one and only begotten Son that whosoever believes in Him shall not perish, but have everlasting life.
    JOHN 3:16

5. God is a God of justice, love, and mercy. Knowing Him, I believe that when children die before reaching an age of accountability—an age when they are mentally and psychologically able to choose to name Jesus as their Savior—then God will, out of His abundant grace and mercy, welcome those children into heaven for eternity. (Book Page 29)

But now he is dead; why should I fast? Can I bring him back again? I shall go to him, but he shall not return to me.
    – KING DAVID IN 2 SAMUEL 12:23 AFTER HIS SON DIED

Assuredly, I say to you, unless you are converted and become as little children, you will by no means enter the kingdom of heaven. Therefore whoever humbles himself as this little child is the greatest in the kingdom of heaven.
    – JESUS IN MATTHEW 18:3-4

But Jesus said, "Let the little children come to Me, and do not forbid them, for of such is the kingdom of heaven."
    MATTHEW 19:14

6. Your child and my child in heaven really don't care any longer about the things of this earth. They live life abundantly in heaven, and they want us to live abundantly here on earth, but ultimately—in God's perfect timing—they want us to join them in paradise. Look at this very important message of Lazarus and the rich man as written in the book of Luke: (Book Page 30)

> *There was a certain rich man who was clothed in purple and fine linen and fared sumptuously every day. But there was a certain beggar named Lazarus, full of sores, who was laid at his gate, desiring to be fed with the crumbs which fell from the rich man's table. Moreover the dogs came and licked his sores. So it was that the beggar died, and was carried by the angels to Abraham's bosom. The rich man also died and was buried. And being in torments in Hades, he lifted up his eyes and saw Abraham afar off, and Lazarus in his bosom.*
>
> *Then he cried and said, "Father Abraham, have mercy on me, and send Lazarus that he may dip the tip of his finger in water and cool my tongue; for I am tormented in this flame." But Abraham said, "Son, remember that in your lifetime you received your good things, and likewise Lazarus evil things; but now he is comforted and you are tormented. And besides all this, between us and you there is a great gulf fixed, so that those who want to pass from here to you cannot, nor can those from there pass to us."*
>
> *Then he said, "I beg you therefore, father, that you would send him to my father's house, for I have five brothers, that he may testify to them, lest they also come to this place of torment." Abraham said to him, "They have Moses and the prophets; let them hear them." And he said, "No, father Abraham; but if one goes to them from the dead, they will repent." But he said to him, "If they do not hear Moses and the prophets, neither will they be persuaded though one rise from the dead."*
>
> LUKE 16:19-31

7. I knew God was out there somewhere, but I was quite content doing whatever pleased me; the lusts of the flesh were my gods. Ephesians 2:1-3 describes my life before coming to God: (Book Page 33)

> And you He *made alive, who were dead in trespasses and sins, in which you once walked according to the course of this world, according to the prince of the power of the air, the spirit who now*

works in the sons of disobedience, among whom also we all once conducted ourselves in the lusts of our flesh, fulfilling the desires of the flesh and of the mind, and were by nature children of wrath, just as the others.

8. Only later would I learn the truth that all my works and efforts to make it into heaven were fruitless. Only later would I discover that only by God's grace and our faith are we saved, that I simply had to receive what He offered. Scripture says it best: (Book Page 33)

> *But God, who is rich in mercy, because of His great love with which He loved us, even when we were dead in trespasses, made us alive together with Christ (by grace you have been saved), and raised us up together, and made us sit together in the heavenly places in Christ Jesus, that in the ages to come He might show the exceeding riches of His grace in His kindness toward us in Christ Jesus. For by grace you have been saved through faith, and that not of yourselves; it is the gift of God, not of works, lest anyone should boast. For we are His workmanship, created in Christ Jesus for good works, which God prepared beforehand that we should walk in them.*
>
> EPHESIANS 2:4-10

9. Satan had been the leader over all of worship in heaven, but he and one-third of the angels rebelled against God and were cast out. Yet Satan is busy on Planet Earth. Hear the words of Peter: (Book Page 36)

> *Cast all your anxiety on him because he cares for you. Be self-controlled and alert. Your enemy the devil prowls around like a roaring lion looking for someone to devour. Resist him, standing firm in the faith, because you know that your brothers throughout the world are undergoing the same kind of sufferings.*
>
> 1 PETER 5:7-9

(Related Scripture verses can be found in appendix E, section 1.)

10. I knew Linda had something real—she had the peace and faith I was missing in my life, peace and faith I had never seen before—and I wanted it. Isaiah 40:31 describes it this way: (Book Page 37)

But those who wait on the LORD
Shall renew their strength;
They shall mount up with wings like eagles,
They shall run and not be weary,
They shall walk and not faint.

11. I mistakenly believed that I could earn a place in heaven by doing good works and being a good person. Later I learned that's not how it works. (Book Page 39)

    For it is by grace you have been saved, through faith—and this not from yourselves, it is the gift of God—not by works, so that no one can boast. For we are God's workmanship, created in Christ Jesus to do good works, which God prepared in advance for us to do.

    EPHESIANS 2:8-10 NIV

    (Related Scripture verses can be found in appendix E, section 2.)

12. Jesus Himself said there is only one way to God the Father, only one way into heaven: (Book Page 39)

    "Let not your heart be troubled; you believe in God, believe also in Me. In My Father's house are many mansions; if it were not so, I would have told you. I go to prepare a place for you. And if I go and prepare a place for you, I will come again and receive you to Myself; that where I am, there you may be also. And where I go you know, and the way you know."

    Thomas said to Him, "Lord, we do not know where You are going, and how can we know the way?"

    Jesus said to him, "I am the way, the truth, and the life. No one comes to the Father except through Me."

    JOHN 14:1-6

13. When we see our loved ones again, it will be as if no time has passed, and we will no longer remember all the sorrow, tears, heartache, and pain we felt here on earth. (Book Page 41)

    I heard a loud voice from heaven saying, "Behold, the tabernacle of God is with men, and He will dwell with them, and they shall be His people. God Himself will be with them and be their God. And God will wipe away every tear from their eyes; there shall be no more death, nor sorrow, nor crying. There shall be no more

pain, for the former things have passed away."
    *Then He who sat on the throne said, "Behold, I make all
things new." And He said to me, "Write, for these words are true
and faithful."*
    REVELATION 21:3-5

14. I know that I will tearfully share this story of Marky's death through
    ministry for the rest of my life, but I will also share with tears of joy
    the hope I have in God: (Book Page 42)

    *Those who sow in tears
        Shall reap in joy.
    He who continually goes forth weeping,
        Bearing seed for sowing,
        Shall doubtless come again with rejoicing,
        Bringing his sheaves with him.*
    PSALM 126:5-6

15. I know all too well that the valley of the shadow of death is a very real
    place, and I know that God walked me through it, especially during
    the three days after Marky's passing. I was definitely in that valley—
    and maybe you are there now—but I was not alone and neither are
    you. God was with me, and He is there for you and with you as well.
    (Book Page 42)

    *The LORD is my shepherd;
        I shall not want.
    He makes me to lie down in green pastures;
        He leads me beside the still waters.
    He restores my soul;
        He leads me in the paths of righteousness
        For His name's sake.
    Yea, though I walk through the valley of the shadow of death,
        I will fear no evil;
        For You are with me;
        Your rod and Your staff, they comfort me.
    You prepare a table before me in the presence of my enemies;
        You anoint my head with oil;
        My cup runs over.
    Surely goodness and mercy shall follow me
        All the days of my life;*

And I will dwell in the house of the LORD
Forever.
PSALM 23

(Related Scripture verses can be found in appendix E, section 3.)

16. When we are in one of life's horrifying and painful valleys, you and I have a choice to make. Will we choose to make God our refuge, fortress, strength, and hope? (Book Page 43)

He who dwells in the secret place of the Most High
Shall abide under the shadow of the Almighty.
I will say of the LORD, "He is my refuge and my fortress;
My God, in Him I will trust."

Surely He shall deliver you from the snare of the fowler
And from the perilous pestilence.
He shall cover you with His feathers,
And under His wings you shall take refuge;
His truth shall be your shield and buckler.
You shall not be afraid of the terror by night,
Nor of the arrow that flies by day,
Nor of the pestilence that walks in darkness,
Nor of the destruction that lays waste at noonday.
PSALM 91:1-6

(The entire psalm can be found in appendix E, section 5.)

17. In his letter to the Ephesians, the apostle Paul—soon to be beheaded in Rome—described the battle we believers face as well as our need for the whole armor of God: (Book Page 45)

Finally, my brethren, be strong in the Lord and in the power
of His might. Put on the whole armor of God, that you may be
able to stand against the wiles of the devil. For we do not wrestle
against flesh and blood, but against principalities, against powers,
against the rulers of the darkness of this age, against spiritual
hosts of wickedness in the heavenly places. Therefore take up the
whole armor of God, that you may be able to withstand in the evil
day, and having done all, to stand.
EPHESIANS 6:10-13

(The entire chapter can be found in appendix E, section 7.)

For though we walk in the flesh, we do not war according to the flesh. For the weapons of our warfare are not carnal but mighty in God for pulling down strongholds, casting down arguments and every high thing that exalts itself against the knowledge of God, bringing every thought into captivity to the obedience of Christ.

    2 CORINTHIANS 10:3-5

18. From prison, the apostle Paul wrote to Timothy: (Book Page 47)

You therefore must endure hardship as a good soldier of Jesus Christ. No one engaged in warfare entangles himself with the affairs of this life, that he may please him who enlisted him as a soldier.

    2 TIMOTHY 2:3-4

(The entire chapter can be found in appendix E, section 8.)

19. It was as if my life were moving in slow motion and my body was totally numb. The pain I felt is described in the book of Job. His life was turned upside-down after every member of his entire family died: (Book Page 60)

Yet when I hoped for good, evil came;
    when I looked for light, then came darkness.
The churning inside me never stops;
    days of suffering confront me.

    JOB 30:26-27 NIV

20. When you suffer the death of a child, Satan continuously throws at you thoughts about what you could have or should have done. Those flaming arrows or fiery darts can cut deep and do great harm to our soul and inner being. (Book Page 70)

Finally, be strong in the Lord and in his mighty power. Put on the full armor of God so that you can take your stand against the devil's schemes. For our struggle is not against flesh and blood, but against the rulers, against the authorities, against the powers of this dark world and against the spiritual forces of evil in the heavenly realms. Therefore put on the full armor of God, so that when the day of evil comes, you may be able to stand your ground, and after you have done everything, to stand. Stand firm then, with the belt of truth buckled around your waist, with the breast-plate of righteousness in place, and with your feet fitted with the readiness that comes from the gospel of peace. In addition to all this, take up the shield of faith, with which you can extinguish all the flaming arrows of the evil one. Take the helmet of salvation and the sword of the Spirit, which is the word of God.

EPHESIANS 6:10-17 NIV

21. You cannot lose your salvation once you have claimed Jesus as Savior and Lord and you have been adopted by Father God into His family. (Book Page 71)

And I give them eternal life, and they shall never perish; neither shall anyone snatch them out of My hand. My Father, who has given them to Me, is greater than all; and no one is able to snatch them out of My Father's hand.

– JESUS IN JOHN 10:28-29

22. *"This righteousness from God comes through faith in Jesus Christ to all who believe. There is no difference, for all have sinned and fall short of the glory of God, and are justified freely by His grace through the redemption that came by Christ Jesus"*

ROMANS 3:22-24 NIV (Book Page 76)

23. Read what the writer of the book of Hebrews explains: (Book Page 77)

If we deliberately keep on sinning after we have received the knowledge of the truth, no sacrifice for sins is left, but only a fearful expectation of judgment and of raging fire that will consume the enemies of God. Anyone who rejected the law of Moses died without mercy on the testimony of two or three witnesses. How much more severely do you think a man deserves to be punished who has trampled the Son of God under foot, who has treated as an unholy thing the blood of the covenant that sanctified him, and who has insulted the Spirit of grace? For we know him who said, "It is mine to avenge; I will repay," and again, "The Lord will judge his people." It is a dreadful thing to fall into the hands of the living God.

HEBREWS 10:26-31 NIV

24. Jesus said it best to the religious hypocrites that would ultimately have Him crucified: *"Woe to you, teachers of the law and Pharisees, you hypocrites! You shut the door of the kingdom of heaven in people's faces. You yourselves do not enter, nor will you let those enter who are trying to"*

MATTHEW 23:13-14

(Jesus' entire message to the church leaders is in appendix E, section 10.)

We also see Jesus's actions speak of His rage against the hypocrisy and legalism of His day—and He was hardly acting wimpy or weak!

When they arrived back in Jerusalem, Jesus entered the Temple and began to drive out the people buying and selling animals for sacrifices. He knocked over the tables of the money changers and the chairs of those selling doves, and he stopped everyone from using the Temple as a marketplace. He said to them, "The Scriptures declare, 'My Temple will be called a house of prayer for all nations,' but you have turned it into a den of thieves."
    When the leading priests and teachers of religious law heard what Jesus had done, they began planning how to kill him. *But they were afraid of him because the people were so amazed at his teaching.*

MARK 11:15-18 NLT, EMPHASIS ADDED

These religious leaders of the day—the Sadducees and Pharisees—were the ones who handed Jesus over to the Roman governor Pontius Pilate. When these men demanded that Jesus be executed on the cross, Pilate issued the order, but he stated, "I find no fault with this man. . . . I am innocent of this man's blood" (Mark 11:17).

Pilate was, however, far from innocent in the horrible beating, whipping, and bloody abuse Jesus suffered just prior to His crucifixion. (Mel Gibson's movie *The Passion* is a vivid depiction much of what that abuse must have been like. I cry any time I really, truly, deeply think of how Jesus was beaten and suffered such excruciating pain for me—and for you.) Yet Pilate raised a good question for any rational thinker to wrestle with: What did Jesus do to deserve that kind punishment and public crucifixion? What was His crime? Jesus had upset the religious leaders of the day, and their putting Him to death was a fulfillment of His purpose on this earth: to die on behalf of humanity's sin. God's sovereign will was fulfilled and our salvation secured. (Book Page 77)

25. The enemy tried to come at me again just as intensely as he had the
night before, but I was gaining strength. I had the Omnipotent Creator of the universe and of everything in it on my side, and nothing
compares to His power and might. (Book Page 78)

Even to your old age and gray hairs
   I am he, I am he who will sustain you.
   I have made you and I will carry you;
   I will sustain you and I will rescue you.

To whom will you compare me or count me equal?
   To whom will you liken me that we may be compared?"

   Remember the former things, those of long ago;
      I am God, and there is no other;
      I am God, and there is none like me.

   I make known the end from the beginning,
      from ancient times, what is still to come.
      I say: My purpose will stand,
      and I will do all that I please.

   Isaiah 46:4-5, 9-10 NIV

26. Humbled by pain as well as by God's amazing presence with me, I
was profoundly humbled. I had a contrite spirit, a broken heart, and
a willingness to serve my God. After all, He had revealed His love
to me in my brokenness in a way far greater than I ever could have
asked or imagined. (Book Page 80)

The LORD is near to those who have a broken heart,
   And saves such as have a contrite spirit.

   Psalm 34:18

The sacrifices of God are a broken spirit,
   A broken and a contrite heart—
   These, O God, You will not despise.

   Psalm 51:17

Has not my hand made all these things,
   and so they came into being?"
   declares the LORD.
   "This is the one I esteem:
   he who is humble and contrite in spirit,
   and trembles at my word."

   Isaiah 66:2 NIV

> The curse of the LORD is on the house of the wicked,
> But He blesses the home of the just.
> Surely He scorns the scornful,
> But gives grace to the humble.
> The wise shall inherit glory,
> But shame shall be the legacy of fools.
>
> PROVERBS 3:33-35

27. I believe our earthly bodies are simply a vessel to hold our soul and spirit. That was not my son lying there; he was alive in heaven, living his new chapter of eternal life abundantly. (Book Page 81)

Now we know that if the earthly tent we live in is destroyed, we have a building from God, an eternal house in heaven, not built by human hands. Meanwhile we groan, longing to be clothed with our heavenly dwelling, because when we are clothed, we will not be found naked. For while we are in this tent, we groan and are burdened, because we do not wish to be unclothed but to be clothed with our heavenly dwelling, so that what is mortal may be swallowed up by life. Now it is God who has made us for this very purpose and has given us the Spirit as a deposit, guaranteeing what is to come.

2 CORINTHIANS 5:1-5 NIV

28. Most of the time I had the peace Jesus had promised. (Book Page 82)

Peace I leave with you; my peace I give you. I do not give to you as the world gives. Do not let your hearts be troubled and do not be afraid.

JOHN 14:27 NIV

29. Salvation is indeed reason for joy on earth and in the heavens. (Book Page 97)

I tell you that in the same way there will be more rejoicing in heaven over one sinner who repents than over ninety-nine righteous persons who do not need to repent....
In the same way, I tell you, there is rejoicing in the presence of the angels of God over one sinner who repents.

LUKE 15:7, 10 NIV

30. It's no surprise that Marky's eyes had changed. Hear God's truth about what our eyes reveal: (Book Page 105)

Your eye is a lamp that provides light for your body. When your eye is good, your whole body is filled with light. But when your eye is bad, your whole body is filled with darkness. And if the light you think you have is actually darkness, how deep that darkness is!

– JESUS IN MATTHEW 6:22-23 NLT

31. The Lord is stronger than sin and death, and He promises— and He can and He does—bring good out of all that Satan means for evil. (Book Page 112)

Now He who searches the hearts knows what the mind of the Spirit is, because He makes intercession for the saints according to the will of God.

And we know that all things work together for good to those who love God, to those who are the called according to His purpose. For whom He foreknew, He also predestined to be conformed to the image of His Son, that He might be the firstborn among many brethren.

ROMANS 8:27-29, EMPHASIS ADDED

(All of Romans 8 can be found in appendix E, section 4.)

32. This ministry was birthed in tears. (Book Page 115)

Those that sow in tears
Shall reap in joy.
He who continually goes forth weeping,
Bearing seed for sowing,
Shall doubtless come again rejoicing,
Bringing his sheaves with him.

PSALM 126:5-6 NIV

33. God's sovereignty through time and in every aspect of your life and mine is a source of hope, comfort, and peace. (Book Page 116)

For you created my inmost being;
  you knit me together in my mother's womb.

I praise you because I am fearfully and wonderfully made;
your works are wonderful,
I know that full well.

PSALM 139:13-14 NIV

So do not be ashamed to testify about our Lord, or ashamed of me
his prisoner. But join with me in suffering for the gospel, by the
power of God, who has saved us and called us to a holy life—not
because of anything we have done but because of his own purpose
and grace. This grace was given us in Christ Jesus before the
beginning of time, but it has now been revealed through the ap-
pearing of our Savior, Christ Jesus, who has destroyed death and
has brought life and immortality to light through the gospel.

2 TIMOTHY 1:8-10 NIV

34. The writer of the Hebrews says this: (Book Page 121) *"Keep on loving*
each other as brothers and sisters. Don't forget to show hospitality to strang-
ers, for some who have done this have entertained angels without realizing
it" (13:1-2 NLT).

35. Here is one statement of that promise: (Book Page 121)

This is what was spoken by the prophet Joel:
"In the last days, God says,
I will pour out my Spirit on all people.
Your sons and daughters will prophesy,
your young men will see visions,
your old men will dream dreams.
Even on my servants, both men and women,
I will pour out my Spirit in those days,
and they will prophesy."

ACTS 2:16-18 NIV

36. Jesus explained that very fact to His disciples: (Book Page 123)

Because of your unbelief; for assuredly, I say to you, if you have
faith as a mustard seed, you will say to this mountain, 'Move
from here to there,' and it will move; and nothing will be impos-
sible for you. However, this kind does not go out except by prayer
and fasting.

MATTHEW 17:20-22

37. In September 2009, on the eve of the release of this book, Dena and I attended an awesome conference on classic Christianity. Leaders Bob George and Bob Christopher of People to People Ministries addressed in detail the finished work of Jesus Christ, and my understanding of what true Christianity should be was confirmed and greatly enhanced. We read Bob George's *Classic Christianity*, which I highly recommend. Their Web site is www.realanswers.net. Below are some important lessons Dena and I learned at the conference, and the statements are based on my notes and conversations with both Mr. George and Mr. Christopher:

We cannot produce love through human effort; we only bear the fruit of love as we abide in the vine of Christ Jesus. We need to be obedient and to learn to love like Jesus loved us. If we try to live out the love of God in our own power, we will fall flat on our face, feel frustrated, and, quite possibly, eventually give up on Christianity. Bob George and People to People Ministries have over thirty years of experience working with bound up, legalistic souls that were heaped with the impossibly heavy burden of man-made religion. We all can truly experience freedom once we realize two basic truths: it is impossible to live the Christian life by our own efforts, and our only role is to abide in the One who can.

Jesus teaches this: (Book Page 125)

I am the true vine, and my Father is the gardener. He cuts off every branch in me that bears no fruit, while every branch that does bear fruit he prunes so that it will be even more fruitful. You are already clean because of the word I have spoken to you. Remain in me, and I will remain in you. No branch can bear fruit by itself; it must remain in the vine. Neither can you bear fruit unless you remain in me.

I am the vine; you are the branches. If a man remains in me and I in him, he will bear much fruit; apart from me you can do nothing. If anyone does not remain in me, he is like a branch that is thrown away and withers; such branches are picked up, thrown into the fire and burned. If you remain in me and my words remain in you, ask whatever you wish, and it will be given you. This is to my Father's glory, that you bear much fruit, showing yourselves to be my disciples.

JOHN 15:1-8 NIV

Again, I knew I could never obey God's commands, statutes, decrees, and laws in my own strength. But we can obey when, by abiding in Him and trusting in Him, we draw on His strength. Then He can and will do His work in us and through our lives.

38. Here is Jesus' statement: (Book Page 125) *"Enter through the narrow gate. For wide is the gate and broad is the road that leads to destruction, and many enter through it. But small is the gate and narrow the road that leads to life, and only a few find it."*
    MATTHEW 7:13-14

39. Consider the amazing work of our Creator God! (Book Page 131)

    For You formed my inward parts;
       You covered me in my mother's womb.
    I will praise You, for I am fearfully *and* wonderfully made;
       Marvelous are Your works,
       And *that* my soul knows very well.
    My frame was not hidden from You,
       When I was made in secret,
       And skillfully wrought in the lowest parts of the earth.
    PSALM 139:13-15

40. Find comfort in this truth. After all, we don't want a God whom we finite human beings can totally figure out! (Book Page 132)

    "For My thoughts are not your thoughts,
       Nor are your ways My ways," says the LORD.
    "For as the heavens are higher than the earth,
       So are My ways higher than your ways,
       And My thoughts than your thoughts."
    ISAIAH 55:8-9

41. The following scripture, for instance, had a major impact on my "social mission" to the poor: (Book Page 137)

    "When the Son of Man comes in his glory, and all the angels with him, he will sit on his throne in heavenly glory. All the nations will be gathered before him, and he will separate the people one from another as a shepherd separates the sheep from the goats. He will put the sheep on his right and the goats on his left."

Then the King will say to those on his right, "Come, you who are blessed by my Father; take your inheritance, the kingdom prepared for you since the creation of the world. For I was hungry and you gave me something to eat, I was thirsty and you gave me something to drink, I was a stranger and you invited me in, I needed clothes and you clothed me, I was sick and you looked after me, I was in prison and you came to visit me."

Then the righteous will answer him, "Lord, when did we see you hungry and feed you, or thirsty and give you something to drink?"

"When did we see you a stranger and invite you in, or needing clothes and clothe you? When did we see you sick or in prison and go to visit you?"

The King will reply, "I tell you the truth, whatever you did for one of the least of these brothers of mine, you did for me."

Then he will say to those on his left, "Depart from me, you who are cursed, into the eternal fire prepared for the devil and his angels. For I was hungry and you gave me nothing to eat, I was thirsty and you gave me nothing to drink, I was a stranger and you did not invite me in, I needed clothes and you did not clothe me, I was sick and in prison and you did not look after me."

They also will answer, "Lord, when did we see you hungry or thirsty or a stranger or needing clothes or sick or in prison, and did not help you?"

He will reply, "I tell you the truth, whatever you did not do for one of the least of these, you did not do for me."

"Then they will go away to eternal punishment, but the righteous to eternal life."

MATTHEW 25:31-46 NIV

42. Another passage that changed me dramatically was 1 John 3:16-24: (Book Page 137)

This is how we know what love is: Jesus Christ laid down his life for us. And we ought to lay down our lives for our brothers. If anyone has material possessions and sees his brother in need but has no pity on him, how can the love of God be in him? Dear children, let us not love with words or tongue but with actions and in truth. This then is how we know that we belong to the truth, and how we set our hearts at rest in his presence whenever our hearts condemn us. For God is greater than our hearts, and he knows everything.

Dear friends, if our hearts do not condemn us, we have con-
fidence before God and receive from him anything we ask because
we obey his commands and do what pleases him. And this is his
command: to believe in the name of his Son, Jesus Christ, and to
love one another as he commanded us. Those who obey his com-
mands live in him, and he in them. And this is how we know that
he lives in us: We know it by the Spirit he gave us.

43. Romans 8:37-39 (NIV) promises that nothing can separate us from the love of God. (Book Page 137)

> *No, in all these things we are more than conquerors through him*
> *who loved us. For I am convinced that neither death nor life,*
> *neither angels nor demons, neither the present nor the future,*
> *nor any powers, neither height nor depth, nor anything else in all*
> *creation, will be able to separate us from the love of God that is in*
> *Christ Jesus our Lord.*

(All of Romans 8 can be found in appendix E, section 4.)

44. The following passage is a dialogue between the prophet Daniel and the angel who had been released to take a message to Daniel during his twenty-one-day fast. This angel had to battle in the heavenly regions before being able to answer Daniel's prayers. (Book Page 139)

> *Then he continued, "Do not be afraid, Daniel. Since the first*
> *day that you set your mind to gain understanding and to humble*
> *yourself before your God, your words were heard, and I have come*
> *in response to them. But the prince of the Persian kingdom re-*
> *sisted me twenty-one days. Then Michael, one of the chief princes,*
> *came to help me, because I was detained there with the king of*
> *Persia."*

> DANIEL 10:12-13

(More passages addressing these battles can be found in appendix E, section 11.)

45. Please see information at endnote 24. (Book Page 149)

The Devastating Epidemic of Clergy Abuse

According to the 2002 Southern Baptist Convention, "clergy sexual abuse (CSA) has reached horrific proportions in many churches today." This serious problem is not limited to any one denomination; it can be found among church leaders throughout the Christian community. Its occurrence surely grieves God, and the enemy seizes each incident as a tool of destruction that works from within the body of Christ.

The Hope of Survivors is a worldwide ministry of compassion providing support, hope, and encouragement to victims of pastoral/clergy sexual abuse and misconduct. It was founded by Steve and Samantha Nelson in December 2002. Victims but survivors of CSA, the Nelsons have helped thousands of victims—including our family. We will be forever grateful to these two unselfish servants of the Lord. You can learn more about CSA at www.TheHopeOfSurvivors.com.

VICTIMS OF ABUSE

Victims of any type of abuse want three things: the truth told, the abuse to stop for themselves and others, and a policy put in place so it can never happen again.

The abuse we as a family suffered at the hands of this pastor and his church leaders was devastating. No one could ever have been prepared for an attack of this magnitude, let alone from within the church. Each one of us was severely wounded emotionally and spiritually. Mark, Jr., never fully recovered from this abuse, from witnessing the abuse, devastation, and near destruction of the family he loved.

I will not give Satan any greater place in this book because it is my heart's desire to give God glory. Yet, as painful as this experience has been, we as a family share our experiences to offer hope and healing to others who have walked or will walk the same path. Today we stand firmly together as a family, and we love the Lord with all our hearts. We are survivors of clergy sexual abuse and the church's collusion in the attempted cover-up of that abuse. Mark, Jr., however, was not. My son was never quite the same, nor did he fully recover. We tried several counselors and made many efforts to help him. But, in the end, God chose to take him home and free him from his pain. I no longer question that and fully trust God in all things.

I plan on addressing this very serious issue in a later book, and then I'll fully address details of our abuse and the church's collusion. The fact is that literally thousands and thousands of people are victims or collateral victims of clergy sexual abuse. The truth must be told about this abuse and the dark secret that lurks silently within the church brought to light.

If you are a victim, directly or indirectly, please hear me: you cannot afford to make a decision that will impact your eternal future based on your hurt or on the hypocrisy of sinful human beings. Read that again: you cannot afford to make a decision that will impact your eternal future based on your hurt or on the hypocrisy of sinful human beings.

So I plead with you to get a Bible and learn about Jesus. Read the Gospels of Matthew, Mark, Luke, and John and let God's Spirit help you see Jesus correctly. Again, don't let the hurt you've experienced as a result of man's deception keep you from discovering for yourself who the real Jesus Christ truly is. And as you get to know about Him, you will see that no one has ever been hurt or betrayed in a worse manner by the church—by the religious people of the day—than Jesus Christ Himself. He understands your CSA experience and disillusionment with the institutional church. May that truth encourage you as you get to know Jesus. After all, your eternal future depends on you knowing the truth about who Jesus truly is—and on knowing Him personally as Savior and Lord.

It is no wonder that many people run from "church" as they know it. I myself ran from what I thought the church was for thirty-nine years, until that day 1997 when I met a true man of God feeding the poor in the housing projects. Then I read about Jesus' life and was forever changed.

TRUE OR FALSE LEADERS?

You may be wondering how to know if someone is a true man of God and if you have found a church you can trust. Some leaders may appear holy from the outside, but inwardly, in hidden areas of their lives, they may be steeped with sin and walking in darkness. So do not blindly trust any man or church leader. If and when leaders ever offer counsel, advice, or direction for your life that is not biblical—if their teachings or statements contradict the Word of God—get away from those leaders immediately. As Jesus taught, "You will know them by their fruit." A person's godliness or sinfulness will eventually be evident in words and deeds. Most importantly, what a godly person says and does lines up with the teachings of God's Word.

> *Beware of false prophets, who come to you in sheep's clothing, but inwardly they are ravenous wolves. You will know them by their fruits.*
>
> —JESUS IN MATTHEW 7:15

> *"Woe to the shepherds who destroy and scatter the sheep of My pasture!" says the LORD. Therefore thus says the LORD God of Israel against the shepherds who feed My people: "You have scattered My flock, driven them away, and not attended to them. Behold, I will attend to you for the evil of your doings," says the LORD. "But I will gather the remnant of My flock out of all countries where I have driven them, and bring them back to their folds; and they shall be fruitful and increase. I will set up shepherds over them who will feed them; and they shall fear no more, nor be dismayed, nor shall they be lacking," says the LORD.*
>
> JEREMIAH 23:1-4

(Related passages are listed in appendix E, section 12.)

FORGIVENESS

God is our refuge and our hope if we allow Him to be. My prayer for you, especially if you are a victim of CSA, is that you believe and truly come to know that there is hope and healing in Jesus Christ for every hurting man, woman, and child. Trust in God, abide in Him, lean on His truths, and know that He will see you through one step at a time.

And that is hard to do, if not impossible, if we let unforgiveness and bitterness take root in our lives. The lack of forgiveness is a poison that slowly contaminates and ultimately destroys our spirit and soul. Good and evil cannot occupy our mind, heart, and soul at the same time. Either we forgive or we are bitter. I knew I had to forgive the church and the abusers, but that commandment from the Lord—given for our good—is difficult to obey. Someone much wiser than I told me to pray as Jesus did on the cross: "Father God, forgive them for they do not know what they are doing." I asked God to forgive my abusers when I could not forgive them on my own.

As with any painful experience in life, a lack of forgiveness tries to creep back from time to time. When it does, counter those feelings with truths from the Bible and fill your mind with praise songs. At our Web site www.IveGotHope.com, you can listen to many songs of hope and healing; many of these songs are listed in Appendix D.

Let me close this appendix with a selection from an audiotape I recorded at about 5:00 one morning in 2005 when I woke up in tears after a dream about abuse victims:

It's September 8, 2005, Marky's nineteenth birthday and eight weeks since he entered heaven. The Lord awoke me with a message to shine in His love and make people wonder what I have in Him, to want what I have in Christ, and to speak forth the truth boldly in love.

God awoke me and is still calling to me to pray and to extend a hand to all the victims of clergy sexual abuse and church collusion. Church is to be God's church. It's not supposed to be man's church. It's not a place of "religion," but a place of fellowship with God and worship of Him. It's not about the four walls or how many members, but it's about praising and serving God to the best of the abilities He's given us. In order to heal my marriage and my family, God is saying, I am to reach out with prayer to all victims of CSA.

The abuse my family and other families have experienced is religion at its ugliest. Yet, after all we have been through, I love God and Jesus Christ with all my heart. We couldn't have made it without Christ in our lives. So, in love, my prayers go out to all the victims of CSA. In love, I pray for wounded people who left the church because of the abuser and his leadership.

I also pray that God has restored churches where abuse has taken place and made them healthy, godly churches characterized by love, peace, and kindness. The church is never to be a place where evil is perpetrated against innocent, trusting victims. I pray that these healed churches reach out to the poor, the lost, the hopeless, and the hurting. I pray for the healing of the victims individually and of the church as a whole. I pray that the pain and suffering have ended and that God's love has come forth. I pray that all will walk as Jesus walked on this earth: in love and forgiveness. Amen.

APPENDIX C

Finding Help When You Need It

The enemy loves for us to think that we're alone in our pain... that no one else would understand... and that there is no hope for a better season of life. Stand up against these lies and take a step toward healing by contacting one of the following organizations.

www.hopeofsurvivors.com Themselves victims of the horrible trauma of pastoral sexual abuse, Steve and Samantha Nelson founded Hope of Survivors. True healing—spiritual, emotional, and physical—comes from God alone through the power of His Word. The Nelsons and staff are available to provide encouragement and support via email, written correspondence, phone calls, and conferences.

www.snapnetwork.org We are SNAP, the Survivors Network of those Abused by Priests. We are the nation's largest, oldest and most active support group for women and men wounded by religious authority figures (priests, ministers, bishops, deacons, nuns, brothers, monks, and others). We are an independent and confidential organization, with no connections with the church or church officials. And we are here to help.

www.advocateweb.org People who have been hurt or exploited by a trusted helping professional (doctor, minister, teacher, etc.) can find help and support on AdvocateWeb.

www.suicide.org This Web site will help if you are suicidal, have attempted suicide, or are a suicide survivor. As the site proclaims, "Suicide is NEVER the answer; getting help is the answer."

www.na.org According to its Web site, Narcotics Anonymous is "a non-profit fellowship of men and women for whom drugs have become a major problem. We are recovering addicts who meet regularly to help each other live drug-free.... This is a program of complete abstinence from all drugs, which includes alcohol. Our fellowship focuses on recovery from the disease of addiction; an individual's drug (or drugs) of choice is unimportant." The only requirement for membership is a desire not to use.

www.aa.org According to its Web site, Alcoholics Anonymous "is a fellowship of men and women who share their experience, strength and hope with each other that they may solve their common problem and help others to recover from alcoholism. The only requirement for membership is a desire to stop drinking.... Our primary purpose is to stay sober and help other alcoholics to achieve sobriety."

www.realanswers.net If you've had a negative experience with organized religion and hypocritical religiosity, check out People to People Ministries by visiting this Web site. People to People has helped thousands of people find strength and security on a foundation that can never be shaken, shattered, or cracked. This foundation is the remarkable truth of God's unconditional love and His indisputable grace experienced in a relationship with Jesus Christ. Through its various outreaches, People to People communicates that the Gospel message is not a doctrine to be learned, but a vital truth to be experienced every day.

www.biblegateway.com Choose the language and translation of your choice when you go to Bible Gateway to read or study scripture online. The site allows you to look up passages in scripture according to keywords, phrases, or scripture reference.

HOW CAN I BE SURE I AM GOING TO HEAVEN?

You will spend eternity in heaven once you have said this simple prayer, believing the truth of its words in your heart: "Confess with your mouth the Lord Jesus and believe in your heart that God has raised Him from the dead, [and] you will be saved" (Romans 10:9).

Seem too simple? Receive God's grace and believe this truth. If you have acknowledged in prayer that Jesus is God's Son, who died for your sins and whom God raised from the dead, you are saved from eternal punishment for your sins, and you are going to heaven-guaranteed.

Now my prayer for you is that you will find a godly church and some new friends who share your faith in Christ; that you will read your Bible daily; and that you will tell everyone you know that you have accepted Jesus Christ as your Lord and Savior. I also encourage you to read and re-read God's promises for you, many of which are found in Appendix D. And please send us an e-mail or letter letting us know of your decision to accept Christ or rededicate your life to Him.

Congratulations! By faith, you have securely established your place in heaven. Know that those loved ones who have gone before you—those treasures that await you in heaven—are rejoicing because of your decision that means, in God's perfect time, you will join them one day.

Our Children and Loved Ones in Heaven

I'd like to share some promises and treasures that the Lord has given me concerning our children and other loved ones who have gone before us to heaven. You can also print this page from our Web site at www.IveGotHope.com.

- Our children and loved ones in heaven are true treasures that await us.

- They are in our future, not only in our past.

- In God's presence, where they live life abundantly, a day is like a thousand years and a thousand years like a day. We will be with them in a moment's time, although that moment may be several years here on earth, and we will have eternity with them—and that means forever and ever and ever!

- When we see, hold, hug, and kiss our children again, we will remember no pain, no sorrow, and no time that has passed. It will be as if they were never separated from us.

- God's measure of love for us was revealed in each of the precious days here on earth that He allowed us to spend with our children and other loved ones. And we would give anything—everything—to have just one more day or even hour with them here on earth!

Thankfully—and thanks to our God, the Giver of life *and* life eternal—we have an eternity with our loved ones in heaven.

- God gives three gifts of life: our natural birth, salvation in Jesus Christ (our spiritual birth or rebirth), and eternal life in heaven.

- Our children and other loved ones in heaven want one thing and one thing only: for their parents, family members, and friends to join them in heaven at God's appointed time. Their greatest concern now is about souls—especially the soul of every person they love—being saved and spending eternity with those they love.

- Our loved ones in heaven live the most abundant, most satisfying life possible. Experiencing no more pain, heartache, suffering, they are blessed with a better life than anything we could ever experience on this earth.

- Just as God alone knew the day we are born, He also knows the day we will depart from this earth. Until that day comes and for eternity afterward, He wants a relationship with us, and He offers us that relationship as well as eternal life through His Son, Jesus.

- When our child or loved one who accepted Jesus passed from this earth, that person was instantly in the arms of Jesus.

- We no longer need to say, "I lost my child" or "He/she is dead" because our children/loved ones are not lost. They are in heaven! And they are not dead. They are alive and living life abundantly in heaven. That's why I choose to say, "My son has passed" or "When my son passed." Our loved ones truly have passed over from life on earth to eternal life in heaven!

- Thanks to the death and resurrection of Jesus Christ—because of His victory over the power of sin and death on the cross—the moment we are absent from the body, we are present with Him, our Lord. Our hope and belief in Jesus Christ is the reason why death truly has lost its sting!

- We will stay awake one more hour, knowing that the hour may last thirty or forty more years. We will run the race of faith strongly and wholeheartedly until God chooses to take us home!

- Upon entering heaven—after we kneel before Jesus and confess He is Lord—we will then look to the treasures awaiting us, treasures who are far more precious than silver or gold!

PROMISES FOR HOPE AND HEALING

I encourage you to read the following promises regularly so you can know hope and healing in your heavenly Father and Almighty God. Trust in the Lord and turn to Him to find strength until the day He takes you home where you will be reunited with those treasures who await you in heaven.

Jesus said to her, "I am the resurrection and the life. He who believes in Me, though he may die, he shall live. And whoever lives and believes in Me shall never die."

JOHN 11:25-26

Whoever believes in Him should not perish but have eternal life. For God so loved the world that He gave His only begotten Son, that whoever believes in Him should not perish but have everlasting life. He who believes in the Son has everlasting life; and he who does not believe the Son shall not see life, but the wrath of God abides on him.

JOHN 3:15-16, 36

Lay up for yourselves treasures in heaven, where neither moth nor rust destroys and where thieves do not break in and steal. For where your treasure is, there your heart will be also.

MATTHEW 6:20-21

This is the promise which He Himself made to us: eternal life.

1 JOHN 2:25 NASB

For we know that if our earthly house, this tent, is destroyed, we have a building from God, a house not made with hands, eternal in the heavens.

2 CORINTHIANS 5:1

For we walk by faith, not by sight. We are confident, yes, well pleased rather to be absent from the body and to be present with the Lord.

2 CORINTHIANS 5:7

But Jesus said, "Let the little children come to Me, and do not forbid them; for of such is the kingdom of heaven."

MATTHEW 19:14

My sheep hear My voice, and I know them, and they follow Me. And I give them eternal life, and they shall never perish; neither shall anyone snatch them out of My hand.

JOHN 10:27-28

Jesus said, "And this is the will of Him who sent Me, that everyone who sees the Son and believes in Him may have everlasting life; and I will raise him up at the last day."

JOHN 6:40

And this is eternal life, that they may know You, the only true God, and Jesus Christ whom You have sent.

JOHN 17:3

A faith and knowledge resting on the hope of eternal life, which God, who does not lie, promised before the beginning of time.

TITUS 1:2 NIV

He who believes in the Son has everlasting life; and he who does not believe the Son shall not see life, but the wrath of God abides on him.

JOHN 3:36

I tell you the truth, whoever hears my word and believes Him who sent me has eternal life and will not be condemned; he has crossed over from death to life.

– JESUS IN JOHN 5:24 (EMPHASIS ADDED)

Without God, Jesus Christ, and the Holy Spirit, we are without hope. Hold on to God's promises. – *Mark Canfora Sr.*

Those who sow in tears shall reap in joy.
Psalm 126:5

Mark Canfora Ministries:
A Ministry Birthed in Tears (www.IveGotHope.com)

SONGS OF COMFORT, HOPE, AND HEAVEN

God's truth put to music can bring you peace and comfort in indescribable ways. Enjoy these songs that have been lifelines of promise and hope for me, my family, and my friends.

"Beauty for Ashes" *Crystal Lewis*

"Breath of Heaven" *Dena Canfora* at www.IveGotHope.com

"Cry Out to Jesus" *Third Day*

"Dancing with the Angels" *Monk & Neagle*

"Every Season" *Nichole Nordeman*

"Golden City" *Mal Pope & Julie Costello*

"He Will Carry Me" *Mark Schultz*

"He's My Son" *Mark Schultz*

"Held" *Natalie Grant*

"Homesick" *MercyMe*

"I Will Rise" *Chris Tomlin*

"In the Arms of an Angel" *Sarah McClachlan*

"I've Got Hope" *SM Souljah* at www.Markfest.org

"Praise You in the Storm" *Casting Crowns*

"There Will Be a Day" *Jeremy Camp*

"We Are Not Home Yet" *Steven Curtis Chapman*

"When I Call on Jesus" *Nicole C. Mullen*

"Who Am I" *Casting Crowns*

"With Hope" *Steven Curtis Chapman*

"You" *The Afters*

MUSIC FOR KIDS?

Much of today's secular rap music on the radio and being download-ed from the Internet promotes drug use, alcohol abuse, sexual promiscu-ity, and even murder and killing the police. And this music is a ministry opportunity. Rap music is not going away, so get these CDs and listen to them with your children. Dena and I do—and I'm 51!

The following artists have played at our festivals, and I highly recom-mend that you introduce their music to the youth in your church and home if they currently listen to rap music:

• Jonathan Brewster aka SM (Single-Minded) Souljah is a producer, re-cording engineer, songwriter, artist, and poet. A preacher's son who was saved at age 7, Souljah says the call of God has always been strong on his life. Blessed with a talent and love for music, Souljah discovered early on the passion to record. Born—as Mark Jr. was—on 09/08/86. myspace. com/smsouljah

• Lecrae had the number one gospel album in 2008, the first time ever a hip-hop album has held that position on Billboard's Top Gospel Albums chart in the U.S. Learn more about Lecrae and other artists at www. ReachRecords.com.

• Ryan Vestal (a.k.a. "Gritty") is a rap artist with an urgent mission: to impact the globe with the life-changing gospel of Jesus Christ. Find out more at http://www.myspace.com/repthaking.

• Da Burnin Bush. The name says it all: this man is on fire for God. A gospel rapper from Birmingham, Alabama, Stephen The Burnin Bush has bangin' beats and anointed lyrics that are bound to set you ablaze. Meet him at http://www.myspace.com/daburninbush.

• www.air1.com The Positive Alternative... Listener-supported contemporary Christian music 24/7. Go to the Web site for a listing of Air 1 stations around the country or to stream Air 1 audio. Site also features links to every artist played on Air 1.

• www.klove.com Listener-supported positive and encouraging Christian music 24/7. At the web site, see a listing of K-LOVE stations, stream the audio, and find links to all artists played.

K-LOVE and Air1 broadcast over 600 radio signals from coast to coast. Both networks are owned and operated by Educational Media Foundation, a nonprofit 501 c3.

• www.wayneaudio.com In addition to being on K-LOVE radio weeknights from 6pm -12 midnight Pacific Time all across the USA, Larry Wayne does freelance voice work from his home studio. His is the amazing voice for this book, available on our Web site as an audiobook. Larry has been happily married to his wife, Dean, for 28 years. They have three adult children and seven grandkids. Larry and Dean live in northern California.

"I HEARD MY FATHER PRAY"

Marky's birthday, September 8, 1986

I heard my father pray. . .
    Dear God, let him live,
    One more second . . .
    One more minute . . .
    One more hour . . .
    Let him live, I'll do anything
    Dear God, let him live;

I heard my father pray . . .
    Thank You, God . . . Thank You, God . . .
    He lives on this, his birth day.

Marky's salvation day, October 7, 2000, as he accepted Jesus as Lord and Savior

I heard my father pray . . .
    Thank You, God . . . Thank You, God . . .
    He lives on this, his salvation day.

The phone call from Carly

I heard my father pray . . .
    Why God? Why God?
    Let him live, let him live . . .
    One more second . . .
    One more minute . . .
    One more hour . . .
    Let him live, I'll do anything . . .
    Dear God, let him live.

I heard my father pray . . .
    Why, Lord? Why?

    Eighteen years, ten months, three days . . .
    I let him live . . .

We heard our Father say.

Marky's entry into heaven, July 12, 2005

You asked for his life
And I gave it to you . . .
But now he is with Me . . .
on this glorious day.
We heard our Father say . . .

Thank You, God . . . Thank You . . .
I heard my father pray . . .
Praise You, God . . . Praise You . . .
I heard my father pray...I heard my father pray.

MARK V. CANFORA
JULY 19, 2005, 5:32 A.M.
AS WRITTEN IN MY JOURNAL

More Words of Life

1: SATAN CAST DOWN FROM HEAVEN

Then the seventy returned with joy, saying, "Lord, even the demons are subject to us in Your name."

And Jesus said to them, "I saw Satan fall like lightning from heaven. Behold, I give you the authority to trample on serpents and scorpions, and over all the power of the enemy, and nothing shall by any means hurt you." (Luke 10:17-19)

The great dragon was hurled down—that ancient serpent called the devil, or Satan, who leads the whole world astray. He was hurled to the earth, and his angels with him.

> Then I heard a loud voice in heaven say:
> "Now have come the salvation and the power and the kingdom
> of our God,
>   and the authority of his Christ.
> For the accuser of our brothers,
>   who accuses them before our God day and night,
>   has been hurled down.
> They overcame him
>   by the blood of the Lamb
>   and by the word of their testimony;
>   they did not love their lives so much
>   as to shrink from death.
> REVELATION 12:9-11 NIV

God did not spare angels when they sinned, but sent them to hell, putting them into gloomy dungeons to be held for judgment. (2 Peter 2:4 NIV)

2. GRACE, FAITH, AND DEEDS

For it is by grace you have been saved, through faith—and this not from yourselves, it is the gift of God—not by works, so that no one can boast. For we are God's workmanship, created in Christ Jesus to do good works, which God prepared in advance for us to do.
EPHESIANS 2:8-10

What good is it, my brothers, if a man claims to have faith but has no deeds? Can such faith save him? Suppose a brother or sister is without clothes and daily food. If one of you says to him, "Go, I wish you well; keep warm and well fed," but does nothing about his physical needs, what good is it? In the same way, faith by itself, if it is not accompanied by action, is dead.

But someone will say, "You have faith; I have deeds." Show me your faith without deeds, and I will show you my faith by what I do.

You believe that there is one God. Good! Even the demons believe that—and shudder.

You foolish man, do you want evidence that faith without deeds is useless? Was not our ancestor Abraham considered righteous for what he did when he offered his son Isaac on the altar? You see that his faith and his actions were working together, and his faith was made complete by what he did. And the scripture was fulfilled that says, "Abraham believed God, and it was credited to him as righteousness," and he was called God's friend. You see that a person is justified by what he does and not by faith alone.

In the same way, was not even Rahab the prostitute considered righteous for what she did when she gave lodging to the spies and sent them off in a different direction? As the body without the spirit is dead, so faith without deeds is dead. (James 2:14-26)

3. PSALM 22 NIV

My God, my God, why have you forsaken me?
  Why are you so far from saving me,
    so far from the words of my groaning?

O my God, I cry out by day, but you do not answer,
  by night, and am not silent.

Yet you are enthroned as the Holy One;
  you are the praise of Israel.

In you our fathers put their trust;
  they trusted and you delivered them.

They cried to you and were saved;
  in you they trusted and were not disappointed.

But I am a worm and not a man,
  scorned by men and despised by the people.

All who see me mock me;
  they hurl insults, shaking their heads:

"He trusts in the LORD;
  let the LORD *rescue him.*
  Let him deliver him,
    since he delights in him."

Yet you brought me out of the womb;
  you made me trust in you
    even at my mother's breast.

From birth I was cast upon you;
  from my mother's womb you have been my God.

Do not be far from me,
  for trouble is near
    and there is no one to help.

Many bulls surround me;
strong bulls of Bashan encircle me.

Roaring lions tearing their prey
open their mouths wide against me.

I am poured out like water,
and all my bones are out of joint.
My heart has turned to wax;
it has melted away within me.

My strength is dried up like a potsherd,
and my tongue sticks to the roof of my mouth;
you lay me in the dust of death.

Dogs have surrounded me;
a band of evil men has encircled me,
they have pierced my hands and my feet.

I can count all my bones;
people stare and gloat over me.

They divide my garments among them
and cast lots for my clothing.

But you, O Lord, be not far off;
O my Strength, come quickly to help me.

Deliver my life from the sword,
my precious life from the power of the dogs.

Rescue me from the mouth of the lions;
save me from the horns of the wild oxen.

I will declare your name to my brothers;
in the congregation I will praise you.

You who fear the Lord, praise him!
All you descendants of Jacob, honor him!
Revere him, all you descendants of Israel!

For he has not despised or disdained
the suffering of the afflicted one;

he has not hidden his face from him
but has listened to his cry for help.

From you comes the theme of my praise in the great assembly;
before those who fear you will I fulfill my vows.

The poor will eat and be satisfied;
they who seek the LORD will praise him—
may your hearts live forever!

All the ends of the earth
will remember and turn to the LORD,
and all the families of the nations
will bow down before him,

for dominion belongs to the LORD
and he rules over the nations.

All the rich of the earth will feast and worship;
all who go down to the dust will kneel before him—
those who cannot keep themselves alive.

Posterity will serve him;
future generations will be told about the Lord.

They will proclaim his righteousness
to a people yet unborn—
for he has done it.

4. ROMANS 8 NIV

Therefore, there is now no condemnation for those who are in Christ Jesus, because through Christ Jesus the law of the Spirit of life set me free from the law of sin and death. For what the law was powerless to do in that it was weakened by the sinful nature, God did by sending his own Son in the likeness of sinful man to be a sin offering. And so he condemned sin in sinful man, in order that the righteous requirements of the law might be fully met in us, who do not live according to the sinful nature but according to the Spirit.

Those who live according to the sinful nature have their minds set on what that nature desires; but those who live in accordance with the

Spirit have their minds set on what the Spirit desires. The mind of sinful man is death, but the mind controlled by the Spirit is life and peace; the sinful mind is hostile to God. It does not submit to God's law, nor can it do so. Those controlled by the sinful nature cannot please God.

You, however, are controlled not by the sinful nature but by the Spirit, if the Spirit of God lives in you. And if anyone does not have the Spirit of Christ, he does not belong to Christ. But if Christ is in you, your body is dead because of sin, yet your spirit is alive because of righteousness. And if the Spirit of him who raised Jesus from the dead is living in you, he who raised Christ from the dead will also give life to your mortal bodies through his Spirit, who lives in you.

Therefore, brothers, we have an obligation—but it is not to the sinful nature, to live according to it. For if you live according to the sinful nature, you will die; but if by the Spirit you put to death the misdeeds of the body, you will live, because those who are led by the Spirit of God are sons of God. For you did not receive a spirit that makes you a slave again to fear, but you received the Spirit of sonship. And by him we cry, "Abba, Father." The Spirit himself testifies with our spirit that we are God's children. Now if we are children, then we are heirs—heirs of God and co-heirs with Christ, if indeed we share in his sufferings in order that we may also share in his glory.

I consider that our present sufferings are not worth comparing with the glory that will be revealed in us. The creation waits in eager expectation for the sons of God to be revealed. For the creation was subjected to frustration, not by its own choice, but by the will of the one who subjected it, in hope that the creation itself will be liberated from its bondage to decay and brought into the glorious freedom of the children of God.

We know that the whole creation has been groaning as in the pains of childbirth right up to the present time. Not only so, but we ourselves, who have the firstfruits of the Spirit, groan inwardly as we wait eagerly for our adoption as sons, the redemption of our bodies. For in this hope we were saved. But hope that is seen is no hope at all. Who hopes for what he already has? But if we hope for what we do not yet have, we wait for it patiently.

In the same way, the Spirit helps us in our weakness. We do not know what we ought to pray for, but the Spirit himself intercedes for us with groans that words cannot express. And he who searches our hearts knows the mind of the Spirit, because the Spirit intercedes for the saints in accordance with God's will.

And we know that in all things God works for the good of those who love him, who have been called according to his purpose. For those God foreknew he also predestined to be conformed to the likeness of his Son, that he might be the firstborn among many brothers. And those he predestined, he also called; those he called, he also justified; those he justified, he also glorified.

What, then, shall we say in response to this? If God is for us, who can be against us? He who did not spare his own Son, but gave him up for us all—how will he not also, along with him, graciously give us all things? Who will bring any charge against those whom God has chosen? It is God who justifies. Who is he that condemns? Christ Jesus, who died—more than that, who was raised to life—is at the right hand of God and is also interceding for us. Who shall separate us from the love of Christ? Shall trouble or hardship or persecution or famine or nakedness or danger or sword? As it is written:

"For your sake we face death all day long;
we are considered as sheep to be slaughtered."

No, in all these things we are more than conquerors through him who loved us. For I am convinced that neither death nor life, neither angels nor demons, neither the present nor the future, nor any powers, neither height nor depth, nor anything else in all creation, will be able to separate us from the love of God that is in Christ Jesus our Lord.

5. PSALM 91 NIV

He who dwells in the shelter of the Most High
will rest in the shadow of the Almighty.

I will say of the LORD, *"He is my refuge and my fortress,*
my God, in whom I trust."

Surely he will save you from the fowler's snare
and from the deadly pestilence.

He will cover you with his feathers,
and under his wings you will find refuge;
his faithfulness will be your shield and rampart.

You will not fear the terror of night,
nor the arrow that flies by day,

nor the pestilence that stalks in the darkness,
nor the plague that destroys at midday.

A thousand may fall at your side,
ten thousand at your right hand,
but it will not come near you.

You will only observe with your eyes
and see the punishment of the wicked.

If you make the Most High your dwelling—
even the LORD, who is my refuge-

then no harm will befall you,
no disaster will come near your tent.

For he will command his angels concerning you
to guard you in all your ways;

they will lift you up in their hands,
so that you will not strike your foot against a stone.

You will tread upon the lion and the cobra;
you will trample the great lion and the serpent.

"Because he loves me," says the LORD, "I will rescue him;
I will protect him, for he acknowledges my name.

He will call upon me, and I will answer him;
I will be with him in trouble,
I will deliver him and honor him.

With long life will I satisfy him
and show him my salvation."

6. HEBREWS 4 NIV

Therefore, since the promise of entering his rest still stands, let us be careful that none of you be found to have fallen short of it. For we also have had the gospel preached to us, just as they did; but the message they heard was of no value to them, because those who heard did not combine it with faith. Now we who have believed enter that rest, just as God has said,

"So I declared on oath in my anger,
'They shall never enter my rest.'"

And yet his work has been finished since the creation of the world. For somewhere he has spoken about the seventh day in these words: "And on the seventh day God rested from all his work." And again in the passage above he says, "They shall never enter my rest."

It still remains that some will enter that rest, and those who formerly had the gospel preached to them did not go in, because of their disobedience. Therefore God again set a certain day, calling it Today, when a long time later he spoke through David, as was said before:

"Today, if you hear his voice,
do not harden your hearts."

For if Joshua had given them rest, God would not have spoken later about another day. There remains, then, a Sabbath-rest for the people of God; for anyone who enters God's rest also rests from his own work, just as God did from his. Let us, therefore, make every effort to enter that rest, so that no one will fall by following their example of disobedience.

For the word of God is living and active. Sharper than any double-edged sword, it penetrates even to dividing soul and spirit, joints and marrow; it judges the thoughts and attitudes of the heart. Nothing in all creation is hidden from God's sight. Everything is uncovered and laid bare before the eyes of him to whom we must give account.

Therefore, since we have a great high priest who has gone through the heavens, Jesus the Son of God, let us hold firmly to the faith we profess. For we do not have a high priest who is unable to sympathize with our weaknesses, but we have one who has been tempted in every way, just as we are—yet was without sin. Let us then approach the throne of grace with confidence, so that we may receive mercy and find grace to help us in our time of need.

7. EPHESIANS 6 NIV

Children, obey your parents in the Lord, for this is right. "Honor your father and mother"—which is the first commandment with a promise— "that it may go well with you and that you may enjoy long life on the earth." Fathers, do not exasperate your children; instead, bring them up in the training and instruction of the Lord.

Slaves, obey your earthly masters with respect and fear, and with sincerity of heart, just as you would obey Christ. Obey them not only to win their favor when their eye is on you, but like slaves of Christ, doing the will of God from your heart. Serve wholeheartedly, as if you were serving the Lord, not men, because you know that the Lord will reward everyone for whatever good he does, whether he is slave or free.

And masters, treat your slaves in the same way. Do not threaten them, since you know that he who is both their Master and yours is in heaven, and there is no favoritism with him.

Finally, be strong in the Lord and in his mighty power. Put on the full armor of God so that you can take your stand against the devil's schemes. For our struggle is not against flesh and blood, but against the rulers, against the authorities, against the powers of this dark world and against the spiritual forces of evil in the heavenly realms. Therefore put on the full armor of God, so that when the day of evil comes, you may be able to stand your ground, and after you have done everything, to stand. Stand firm then, with the belt of truth buckled around your waist, with the breastplate of righteousness in place, and with your feet fitted with the readiness that comes from the gospel of peace. In addition to all this, take up the shield of faith, with which you can extinguish all the flaming arrows of the evil one. Take the helmet of salvation and the sword of the Spirit, which is the word of God. And pray in the Spirit on all occasions with all kinds of prayers and requests. With this in mind, be alert and always keep on praying for all the saints.

Pray also for me, that whenever I open my mouth, words may be given me so that I will fearlessly make known the mystery of the gospel, for which I am an ambassador in chains. Pray that I may declare it fearlessly, as I should.

Tychicus, the dear brother and faithful servant in the Lord, will tell you everything, so that you also may know how I am and what I am doing. I am sending him to you for this very purpose, that you may know how we are, and that he may encourage you.

Peace to the brothers, and love with faith from God the Father and the Lord Jesus Christ. Grace to all who love our Lord Jesus Christ with an undying love.

8. 2 TIMOTHY 2

You therefore, my son, be strong in the grace that is in Christ Jesus. And the things that you have heard from me among many witnesses, commit these to faithful men who will be able to teach others also. You therefore must endure hardship as a good soldier of Jesus Christ. No one engaged in warfare entangles himself with the affairs of this life, that he may please him who enlisted him as a soldier. And also if anyone competes in athletics, he is not crowned unless he competes according to the rules. The hardworking farmer must be first to partake of the crops. Consider what I say, and may the Lord give you understanding in all things.

Remember that Jesus Christ, of the seed of David, was raised from the dead according to my gospel, for which I suffer trouble as an evildoer, even to the point of chains; but the word of God is not chained. Therefore I endure all things for the sake of the elect, that they also may obtain the salvation which is in Christ Jesus with eternal glory.

This is a faithful saying:

For if we died with Him,

We shall also live with Him.

If we endure,

We shall also reign with Him.
If we deny Him,

He also will deny us.
If we are faithless,

He remains faithful;

He cannot deny Himself.

Remind them of these things, charging them before the Lord not to strive about words to no profit, to the ruin of the hearers. Be diligent to present yourself approved to God, a worker who does not need to be ashamed, rightly dividing the word of truth. But shun profane and idle babblings, for they will increase to more ungodliness. And their message will spread like cancer. Hymenaeus and Philetus are of this sort, who have strayed concerning the truth, saying that the resurrection is already past; and they overthrow the faith of some. Nevertheless the solid foundation of God stands, having this seal: "The Lord knows those who are His," and, "Let everyone who names the name of Christ depart from iniquity."

But in a great house there are not only vessels of gold and silver, but also of wood and clay, some for honor and some for dishonor. Therefore if anyone cleanses himself from the latter, he will be a vessel for honor, sanctified and useful for the Master, prepared for every good work. Flee also youthful lusts; but pursue righteousness, faith, love, peace with those who call on the Lord out of a pure heart. But avoid foolish and ignorant disputes, knowing that they generate strife. And a servant of the Lord must not quarrel but be gentle to all, able to teach, patient, in humility correcting those who are in opposition, if God perhaps will grant them repentance, so that they may know the truth, and that they may come to their senses and escape the snare of the devil, having been taken captive by him to do his will.

9. ISAIAH 61

The Spirit of the Lord God is upon Me,
 Because the Lord has anointed Me
 To preach good tidings to the poor;
He has sent Me to heal the brokenhearted,
 To proclaim liberty to the captives,
 And the opening of the prison to those who are bound;
To proclaim the acceptable year of the Lord,
 And the day of vengeance of our God;
 To comfort all who mourn,
To console those who mourn in Zion,
 To give them beauty for ashes,
 The oil of joy for mourning,
 The garment of praise for the spirit of heaviness;

That they may be called trees of righteousness,
 The planting of the Lord, that He may be glorified."

And they shall rebuild the old ruins,
 They shall raise up the former desolations,

And they shall repair the ruined cities,
The desolations of many generations.
Strangers shall stand and feed your flocks,
And the sons of the foreigner
Shall be your plowmen and your vinedressers.
But you shall be named the priests of the LORD,
They shall call you the servants of our God.
You shall eat the riches of the Gentiles,
And in their glory you shall boast.

Instead of your shame you shall have double honor,
And instead of confusion they shall rejoice in their portion.
Therefore in their land they shall possess double;
Everlasting joy shall be theirs.

" For I, the LORD, love justice;
I hate robbery for burnt offering;
I will direct their work in truth,
And will make with them an everlasting covenant.
Their descendants shall be known among the Gentiles,
And their offspring among the people.

All who see them shall acknowledge them,
That they are the posterity whom the LORD has blessed."

I will greatly rejoice in the LORD,
My soul shall be joyful in my God;
For He has clothed me with the garments of salvation,
He has covered me with the robe of righteousness,
As a bridegroom decks himself with ornaments,
And as a bride adorns herself with her jewels.
For as the earth brings forth its bud,
As the garden causes the things that are sown in it to spring
forth, So the Lord GOD will cause righteousness and praise to
spring forth before all the nations.

10. MATTHEW 23 NIV

Then Jesus said to the crowds and to his disciples: "The teachers of the law and the Pharisees sit in Moses' seat. So you must obey them and do everything they tell you. But do not do what they do, for they do not practice what they preach. They tie up heavy loads and put them on men's shoulders, but they themselves are not willing to lift a finger to move them.

"Everything they do is done for men to see: They make their phylacteries wide and the tassels on their garments long; They love the place of honor at banquets and the most important seats in the synagogues; they love to be greeted in the marketplaces and to have men call them 'Rabbi.'

"But you are not to be called 'Rabbi,' for you have only one Master and you are all brothers. And do not call anyone on earth 'father,' for you have one Father, and he is in heaven. Nor are you to be called 'teacher,' for you have one Teacher, the Christ. The greatest among you will be your servant. For whoever exalts himself will be humbled, and whoever humbles himself will be exalted.

"Woe to you, teachers of the law and Pharisees, you hypocrites! You shut the kingdom of heaven in men's faces. You yourselves do not enter, nor will you let those enter who are trying to.

"Woe to you, teachers of the law and Pharisees, you hypocrites! You travel over land and sea to win a single convert, and when he becomes one, you make him twice as much a son of hell as you are.

"Woe to you, blind guides! You say, 'If anyone swears by the temple, it means nothing; but if anyone swears by the gold of the temple, he is bound by his oath.' You blind fools! Which is greater: the gold, or the temple that makes the gold sacred? You also say, 'If anyone swears by the altar, it means nothing; but if anyone swears by the gift on it, he is bound by his oath.' You blind men! Which is greater: the gift, or the altar that makes the gift sacred? Therefore, he who swears by the altar swears by it and by everything on it. And he who swears by the temple swears by it and by the one who dwells in it. And he who swears by heaven swears by God's throne and by the one who sits on it.

"Woe to you, teachers of the law and Pharisees, you hypocrites! You give a tenth of your spices—mint, dill and cummin. But you have neglected the more important matters of the law—justice, mercy and faithfulness. You should have practiced the latter, without neglecting the former. You blind guides! You strain out a gnat but swallow a camel.

"Woe to you, teachers of the law and Pharisees, you hypocrites! You clean the outside of the cup and dish, but inside they are full of greed and self-indulgence. Blind Pharisee! First clean the inside of the cup and dish, and then the outside also will be clean.

"Woe to you, teachers of the law and Pharisees, you hypocrites! You are like whitewashed tombs, which look beautiful on the outside but on the inside are full of dead men's bones and everything unclean. In the same way, on the outside you appear to people as righteous but on the inside you are full of hypocrisy and wickedness.

"Woe to you, teachers of the law and Pharisees, you hypocrites! You build tombs for the prophets and decorate the graves of the righteous. And you say, 'If we had lived in the days of our forefathers, we would not have taken part with them in shedding the blood of the prophets.' So you testify against yourselves that you are the descendants of those who murdered the prophets. Fill up, then, the measure of the sin of your forefathers!

"You snakes! You brood of vipers! How will you escape being condemned to hell? Therefore I am sending you prophets and wise men and teachers. Some of them you will kill and crucify; others you will flog in your synagogues and pursue from town to town. And so upon you will come all the righteous blood that has been shed on earth, from the blood of righteous Abel to the blood of Zechariah son of Berekiah, whom you murdered between the temple and the altar. I tell you the truth, all this will come upon this generation.

"O Jerusalem, Jerusalem, you who kill the prophets and stone those sent to you, how often I have longed to gather your children together, as a hen gathers her chicks under her wings, but you were not willing. Look, your house is left to you desolate. For I tell you, you will not see me again until you say, 'Blessed is he who comes in the name of the Lord.'"

11. SPIRITUAL BATTLE IN THE HEAVENLY REALMS

So he [the angel] said, "Do you know why I have come to you? Soon I will return to fight against the prince of Persia, and when I go, the prince of Greece will come; but first I will tell you what is written in the Book of Truth."
DANIEL 10:20-21 NIV

And there was war in heaven. Michael and his angels fought against the dragon, and the dragon and his angels fought back. But he was not strong enough, and they lost their place in heaven.

*The great dragon was hurled down—that ancient serpent called
the devil, or Satan, who leads the whole world astray. He was
hurled to the earth, and his angels with him.*

Then I heard a loud voice in heaven say:

*"Now have come the salvation and the power and the kingdom of
our God,*

*and the authority of his Christ.
For the accuser of our brothers,
    who accuses them before our God day and night,
    has been hurled down.
They overcame him
    by the blood of the Lamb
    and by the word of their testimony;
they did not love their lives so much
    as to shrink from death.
Therefore rejoice, you heavens
    and you who dwell in them!
But woe to the earth and the sea,
    because the devil has gone down to you!
He is filled with fury,
    because he knows that his time is short."*
REVELATION 12:7-12 NIV

*If you make the Most High your dwelling—
    even the LORD, who is my refuge—*

*then no harm will befall you,
    no disaster will come near your tent.*

*For he will command his angels concerning you
    to guard you in all your ways;*

*they will lift you up in their hands,
    so that you will not strike your foot against a stone.*

*You will tread upon the lion and the cobra;
    you will trample the great lion and the serpent.*

*"Because he loves me," says the LORD, "I will rescue him;
    I will protect him, for he acknowledges my name.*

He will call upon me, and I will answer him;
  I will be with him in trouble,
  I will deliver him and honor him.

With long life will I satisfy him
  and show him my salvation."

PSALM 91:9-16 NIV

One day the angels came to present themselves before the LORD, and Satan also came with them. The LORD said to Satan, "Where have you come from?"

Satan answered the LORD, "From roaming through the earth and going back and forth in it."

Then the LORD said to Satan, "Have you considered my servant Job? There is no one on earth like him; he is blameless and upright, a man who fears God and shuns evil."

"Does Job fear God for nothing?" Satan replied. "Have you not put a hedge around him and his household and everything he has? You have blessed the work of his hands, so that his flocks and herds are spread throughout the land. But stretch out your hand and strike everything he has, and he will surely curse you to your face."

The LORD said to Satan, "Very well, then, everything he has is in your hands, but on the man himself do not lay a finger."

Then Satan went out from the presence of the LORD.

JOB 1:6-12 NIV

12. YOU WILL KNOW THEM BY THEIR FRUIT

Beware of false prophets, who come to you in sheep's clothing, but inwardly they are ravenous wolves. You will know them by their fruits. Do men gather grapes from thorn bushes or figs from thistles? Even so, every good tree bears good fruit, but a bad tree bears bad fruit. A good tree cannot bear bad fruit, nor can a bad tree bear good fruit. Every tree that does not bear good fruit is cut down and thrown into the fire. Therefore by their fruits you will know them.

– JESUS IN MATTHEW 7:15-20

Whoever receives one little child like this in My name receives Me. Whoever causes one of these little ones who believe in Me to sin, it would be better for him if a millstone were hung around his neck, and he were drowned in the depth of the sea.

Woe to the world because of offenses! For offenses must come, but woe to that man by whom the offense comes!
  – JESUS IN MATTHEW 18:5-7

Now there was a man of the Pharisees named Nicodemus, a member of the Jewish ruling council. He came to Jesus at night and said, "Rabbi, we know you are a teacher who has come from God. For no one could perform the miraculous signs you are doing if God were not with him."

In reply Jesus declared, "I tell you the truth, no one can see the kingdom of God unless he is born again."

"How can a man be born when he is old?" Nicodemus asked. "Surely he cannot enter a second time into his mother's womb to be born!"

Jesus answered, "I tell you the truth, no one can enter the kingdom of God unless he is born of water and the Spirit. Flesh gives birth to flesh, but the Spirit gives birth to spirit. You should not be surprised at my saying, 'You must be born again.' The wind blows wherever it pleases. You hear its sound, but you cannot tell where it comes from or where it is going. So it is with everyone born of the Spirit."

"How can this be?" Nicodemus asked.

"You are Israel's teacher," said Jesus, "and do you not understand these things? I tell you the truth, we speak of what we know, and we testify to what we have seen, but still you people do not accept our testimony. I have spoken to you of earthly things and you do not believe; how then will you believe if I speak of heavenly things? No one has ever gone into heaven except the one who came from heaven—the Son of Man. Just as Moses lifted up the snake in the desert, so the Son of Man must be lifted up, that everyone who believes in him may have eternal life.

"For God so loved the world that he gave his one and only Son, that whoever believes in him shall not perish but have eternal life. For God did not send his Son into the world to condemn the world, but to save the world through him. Whoever believes in him is not condemned, but whoever does not believe stands condemned already because he has not believed in the name of God's one and only Son. *This is the verdict: Light has come into the world, but men loved* darkness instead of light because their deeds were evil. Everyone who does evil hates the light, and will not come into the light for fear that his deeds will be exposed. But whoever lives by the truth comes into the light, so that it may be seen plainly that what he has done has been done through God."

John 3:1-21 NIV, emphasis added

This is how we know what love is: Jesus Christ laid down his life for us. And we ought to lay down our lives for our brothers. If anyone has material possessions and sees his brother in need but has no pity on him, how can the love of God be in him? Dear children, let us not love with words or tongue but with actions and in truth. This then is how we know that we belong to the truth, and how we set our hearts at rest in his presence whenever our hearts condemn us. For God is greater than our hearts, and he knows everything.

Dear friends, if our hearts do not condemn us, we have confidence before God and receive from him anything we ask, because we obey his commands and do what pleases him. And this is his command: to believe in the name of his Son, Jesus Christ, and to love one another as he commanded us. Those who obey his commands live in him, and he in them. And this is how we know that he lives in us: We know it by the Spirit he gave us.

1 John 3:16-24 NIV

Mr. Canfora's Accomplishments and Services

Mark Canfora Sr. is involved in many areas of expertise besides his passion for sharing this hope and healing message. The following are some of the services he offers:

- Speaking Engagements: www.MarkCanfora.com

- Ministry and Festival Meetings: www.IveGotHope.com

- Real Estate Consultant: www.FractionalRealEstateAdvisors.com

- Real Estate Investments in Panama City Beach, Florida: www.InvestinPCBeach.com

- Families and Friends for a Safe Panama City Beach: www.SafePCB.com

- Author: Mr. Canfora has two more books underway, one addressing clergy sexual abuse and the church and the other, getting priorities right in life.

Without God, Jesus Christ, and the Holy Spirit, we are without hope. Hold on to God's promises. – *Mark Canfora Sr.*

Those who sow in tears shall reap in joy.
Psalm 126:5

Mark Canfora Ministries: A Ministry Birthed in Tears

In Christ's love,
Mark Canfora
2433 Thomas Drive #125
Panama City Beach, Florida 32408
(330) 865-1000

For more information on ordering additional books, Celebration of Life t-shirts, free baseball posters, and becoming a ministry partner, please contact us at our web site: www.IveGotHope.com or e-mail me directly at MarkCanfora@aol. com.

By Dominic Canfora—Illustrator

Print and complete this form to pre-order books by mail

Mark Canfora Ministries
"A Child Died, a Father Cried...and God Answered!"

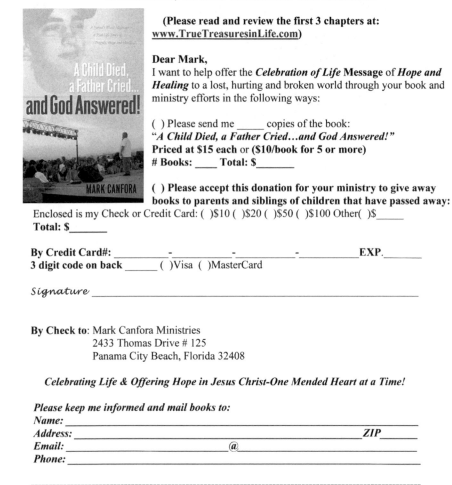

(Please read and review the first 3 chapters at:
www.TrueTreasuresinLife.com)

Dear Mark,
I want to help offer the *Celebration of Life* **Message** of *Hope and Healing* to a lost, hurting and broken world through your book and ministry efforts in the following ways:

( ) Please send me _____ copies of the book:
"A Child Died, a Father Cried...and God Answered!"
Priced at $15 each or ($10/book for 5 or more)
 # Books: _____ Total: $_____

( ) Please accept this donation for your ministry to give away books to parents and siblings of children that have passed away:
Enclosed is my Check or Credit Card: ( )$10 ( )$20 ( )$50 ( )$100 Other( )$_____
Total: $_____

By Credit Card#: _____ - _____ - _____ - _____ **EXP.**_____
3 digit code on back _____ ( )Visa ( )MasterCard

Signature _____

By Check to: Mark Canfora Ministries
2433 Thomas Drive # 125
Panama City Beach, Florida 32408

Celebrating Life & Offering Hope in Jesus Christ-One Mended Heart at a Time!

Please keep me informed and mail books to:
Name: _____
Address: _____ **ZIP**_____
Email: _____ @ _____
Phone: _____

Detach For Your Records:
Mark Canfora Ministries
*2433 Thomas Drive #125 * Panama City Beach, Florida 32408 • 330 865 1000*
www.IveGotHope.com

Amount Donated: $_____ **Date:** _____ **Check #** _____

Print and complete this form to become a Sponsor by mail

Mark Canfora Ministries
"A Child Died, a Father Cried...and God Answered!"

Sponsors and Partners

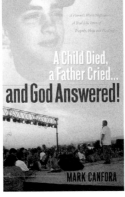

Dear Mark,

I want to help offer the *Celebration of Life* **Message** of *Hope and Healing* to a lost, hurting and broken world through your ministry efforts in the following ways:

( ) Enclosed is my *one time gift* by check:( )$10 ( ) $20 ( )$50 ( )$100 Other( )$_____

( ) Please send me _____ copies of the book: *"A Child Died, a Father Cried...and God Answered!"*
priced at **$15 each** or **($10/book for 5 or more)**
Total: $_____ (Read the first 3 Chapters at: www.TrueTreasuresinLife.com)

( ) **Monthly Partner for One Year**: ( )$10/mo. ( )$20/mo. ( )$50/mo. ( )$100/mo.
Other amount: $_____/month

( ) **On-line Donations and Orders**: www.IveGotHope.com
Secure & Safe

By Credit Card#: _____ - _____ - _____ - _____ EXP._____
3 digit code on back _____ ( )Visa ( )MasterCard

Signature _____

By Check to: Mark Canfora Ministries
2433 Thomas Drive # 125
Panama City Beach, Florida 32408

Celebrating Life & Offering Hope in Jesus Christ-One Mended Heart at a Time!
Please keep me informed:
Name: _____
Address: _____ *ZIP*_____
Email: _____ @_____
Phone: _____

Detach For Your Records:
Mark Canfora Ministries
*2433 Thomas Drive #125 * Panama City Beach, Florida 32408 • 330 865 1000*
www.IveGotHope.com
Amount Donated: $_____Date: _____ Check #_____

*(Left): Mark Canfora Jr.
1986-2005
My son and my treasure in
heaven*

*(Below): Mark Canfora Sr.
and Mark Canfora Jr.,
Christmas 2004*